A WINNING WITNESS

A WINNING WITNESS

GAINES S. DOBBINS

*Professor, Religious Education and
Church Efficiency*

*Southern Baptist Theological Seminary
Louisville, Kentucky*

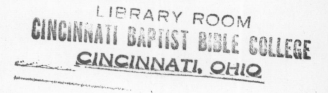

95

NASHVILLE, TENNESSEE
THE SUNDAY SCHOOL BOARD
of the
SOUTHERN BAPTIST CONVENTION

ABOUT THE AUTHOR

Born in the village of Langsdale, Mississippi, reared at Hattiesburg, Mississippi, Gaines Stanley Dobbins attended Mississippi College, where he received the A.B. degree in 1908. After a brief period of teaching in what is now Mississippi Woman's College, he attended Southern Baptist Theological Seminary, Louisville, Kentucky, from which he was graduated with the degree of Th.D. in 1913. In 1925 he received the M.A. degree from Columbia University. He also did graduate work at George Peabody College for Teachers and University of Chicago. His alma mater honored him with D.D. and later with LL.D. degrees.

Following brief pastorates at Gloster and New Albany, Mississippi, Dr. Dobbins was called to the Sunday School Board in an editorial capacity. In 1920 he was elected to the faculty of Southern Baptist Theological Seminary, where he has continued to teach in the fields of religious education and church administration. During the presidency of Dr. John R. Sampey, Dr Dobbins served as treasurer of the seminary. On the death of President Ellis A. Fuller, and until the election of Dr. Duke K. McCall, Dr. Dobbins was interim president. In March, 1953, he was selected by the trustees to become the dean of the newly established School of Religious Education. Dr. Dobbins has written voluminously, being the author of seventeen books and innumerable articles.

Copyright, 1938
The Sunday School Board
of the
Southern Baptist Convention
Nashville, Tennessee

Printed in the United States of America
5.2F543

DIRECTIONS FOR THE TEACHING AND THE STUDY OF THIS BOOK FOR CREDIT

I. *Directions for the Teacher*

1. Ten class periods of forty-five minutes each, or the equivalent, are required for the completion of the book for credit.

2. The teacher of the class is given an award on the book if he requests it.

3. The teacher shall give a written examination covering the subject matter in the textbook, and the student shall make a minimum grade of 70 per cent. The examination may take the form of assigned work to be done between the class sessions, or as a final examination at the end of the course.

Exception: All who attend all of the class sessions; who read the book through by the close of the course; and who, in the judgment of the teacher, do the classwork satisfactorily may be exempted from taking the examination.

4. In the Graded Training Union Study Course, a seal for Course IX, Soul-Winning, is granted to adults for the completion of this book.

Sunday school credit may be elected by the pupil. Application for Sunday school awards should be sent to the state Sunday school department and for Training Union awards to the state Training Union department. These departments will provide the forms for these applications. They should be made in duplicate and both copies sent.

II. *Directions for the Student*

1. In Classwork

(1) The pupil must attend at least six of the ten forty-five minute class periods to be entitled to take the class examination.

(2) The pupil must certify that the textbook has been read. (In rare cases where pupils may find it impracticable to read the book before the completion of the classwork, the teacher may accept a promise to read the book carefully within the next two weeks.)

(3) The pupil must take a written examination, making a minimum grade of 70 per cent. (All who attend all of the class sessions; who read the book through by the close of the course; and who, in the judgment of the teacher, do satisfactory classwork may be exempted from taking the examination.)

2. In Individual Study by Correspondence

Those who for any reason wish to study the book without the guidance of a teacher will use one of the following methods:

(1) Write answers to the questions printed in the books, or

(3) Write a development of the chapter outlines.

If the second method is used, the student will study the book and then with the open book write a development of the chapter outlines.

In either case the student must read the book through.

Students may find profit in studying the text together, but where awards are requested, individual papers are required. Carbon copies or duplicates in any form cannot be accepted.

All written work done by such students on books for Sunday school credit should be sent to the state Sunday school secretary. All of such work done on books for Training Union credit should be sent to the state Training Union secretary.

III. *Interchange of Credits and Awards on Comparable Subjects*

One award, either for Training Union or Sunday school, is granted for completing this book.

J. E. LAMBDIN

Secretary and Editor,
Training Union Department,
Baptist Sunday School Board

C. AUBREY HEARN
Director of the Study Course

CONTENTS

CHRIST MEETING LIFE'S DEEPEST NEEDS

OUTLINE

I. FACING LIFE'S NEEDS

1. The Need of Spiritual Wisdom
2. The Need of Understanding Present-Day Difficulties
3. The Need of Power to Overcome Temptation

II. MISSING LIFE'S MARK

1. The Universal Fact of Sin
2. What Sin Is
3. What Sin Does

III. THE SUPREMACY OF CHRISTIAN CHARACTER

1. What Is Meant by Character?
2. Why Is Christian Character Supremely Important?
3. How Is Christian Character Achieved?
4. Why Is Christian Character Contagious?

CHAPTER I

CHRIST MEETING LIFE'S DEEPEST NEEDS

Evangelism, in the broadest sense, means any testimony borne to another by a Christian with a view to making Christ known and accepted. This witness may be borne in sermon, in song, in personal conversation, by the spoken or the written word, or by the influence of character and conduct.

Southern Baptists believe in and practice evangelism. For many years we have surpassed all other evangelical religious bodies in America in the extent and fruitfulness of our evangelistic efforts. It is to the end that our evangelism may be increasingly honored of God and blessed in its results that these studies have been prepared.

There is a shallow evangelism that would seek primarily to add numbers to the membership of a church. Then there is an evangelism that stirs the emotions and leads to outward profession, but fails to anchor to Christ and his church. Again, there is a dry-eyed intellectual evangelism that presents a system of doctrine and a standard of morals, but lacks power to translate creed and ethic into life. More common is warm-hearted, sensible, doctrinally sound evangelism that is inadequate because it is confined to a brief season of revival, and is not sufficiently preceded and followed by enlistment in service and nurture of the implanted life.

We need for our day a vital evangelism—the living testimony of convincing Christians that Christ is able to save and keep and make strong and useful and happy all who come to God through him. Humanity has many needs, but deeper than any other is the need for a living Lord who can and will save "unto the uttermost." He has saved us, if so be that we are saved. And now he is saying to us who call him Saviour, "Ye shall be my witnesses."

I. Facing Life's Needs

We who go forth as Christian witnesses claim that Christ is sufficient for every need of life. We declare that Christ offers himself and his gospel as the solution of every problem. Does this mean that all trouble vanishes when one becomes a Christian? When you accepted Christ did every doubt and perplexity vanish, and was every lack instantly supplied? Then what do we mean by our claim that Christ is able to supply all our needs? It gets back to the question as to what are our real needs. Is not the great truth that Christ provides all that is necessary to help us meet our own difficulties, rather than that he does it all for us? In the first thirteen verses of the tenth chapter of 1 Corinthians we find a remarkable outline of the needs of life and how these needs are supplied through Christ.

1. *The Need of Spiritual Wisdom*

The people of Israel, saved from the bondage of Egypt by God's mighty hand, underwent some wonderful spiritual experiences. But, as Paul points out, the Israelites themselves did not all learn the meaning of what was happening to them. They knew that they were being guided by the pillar of fire and the cloud; they knew that they passed miraculously through the sea; they knew that the cloud above and the sea all around had completely enveloped them, and thus they had escaped destruction. They were in the midst of great history-making spiritual experiences, all eating of the same spiritual meat and drinking the same spiritual drink. Yet they did not all realize the meaning of these things. They did not understand that all this was a part of God's eternal plan in preparation for the coming of "that spiritual Rock that followed them: and that Rock was Christ."

Could not much the same thing be said about nearly all of us? To us have come many wonderful experiences, to us have been given great and precious privileges, for us and through us God would do mighty things; yet we have not had the spiritual insight to discover God's plans and purposes for our lives. Why? Because we have been contented with our ignorance, and have not been willing to pay the price of gaining spiritual wisdom. Christ and his salvation are the gift of God, but spiritual wisdom to receive and make the best use of this gift is something that we must get by study, humility, obedience, prayer. Is not this spiritual wisdom one of our greatest needs today?

2. The Need of Understanding Present-Day Difficulties

The people of Israel wanted many things they did not have, but they did not want automobiles, radios, electric refrigerators, telephones, electric lights, air-conditioned houses, luxuries from a store near by, high wages for short hours, old-age security pensions, and a score of other things that we moderns think we must have or life is scarcely worth the living.

Many changes are taking place that serve to increase our sense of need. Among these may be mentioned the growth of our towns and cities, bringing great numbers of people together in congested centers. Family life is undergoing radical change, the home largely ceasing to be central in the lives of our people. The replacing of hand work by machinery is having far-reaching effect. The long period of depression, with its hardship and suffering, and the sense of insecurity which it developed among all classes, left its mark on all our lives. The craze for amusement and the lowering of moral standards make the work of the churches more and more difficult. Science has led many people to think they can get along without religion altogether, so that God has less and less place in the thought of multitudes. Thousands are trying to find an escape from their dissatisfaction through the use of alcohol and drugs. The terrible realities of war fall like a blight upon all our boasted civilization. Is it any wonder that we grow confused, as we find ourselves faced with such overwhelming needs as those which confront us in every aspect of modern life?

Is our Christian faith to be thought of as means of escape from all this pressure of need, or shall we through Christ meet these needs by means of our Christian faith? The true Christian is not one who runs away from the problems of life, but one who faces these problems squarely and seeks their solution through study, prayer, effort. A part of Christ's salvation is the ability which he gives to understand the world in which we live and the courage and wisdom which come from him in finding the way out according to the will of God. Do we, deep in our hearts, believe that Jesus Christ is sufficient for every problem of our complex and disturbed world?

3. *The Need of Power to Overcome Temptation*

Perhaps we are saying to ourselves that no other generation has had such temptations as ours. Every now and then we may ask, "I wonder if anybody was ever as sorely tempted and tried as I am?" When we begin to feel like this we need to hear Paul say to us, "There hath no temptation taken you but such as is common to man" (1 Cor. 10:13). Every age has had its special temptations; and every individual has been tempted in some manner. Go over your list of trials, and you will not find one in the entire list that others have not had to undergo. A temptation is an experience of testing, and the need is not to escape temptation but to lay hold on power with which to overcome it.

When temptation comes, and the struggle is on between right and wrong, what is the hope of victory? Paul replies that the all-sufficient source of power is in a faithful God, "who will not suffer you to be tempted above that ye are able; but will with the temptation also make a way to escape, that ye may be able to bear it."

Pressing upon us from every side are these strong temptations—to idolatry, to impurity, to pride, to murmuring and discontent. What is the supreme need? Not some power to remove the temptations, but the presence of God in Christ giving victory over the temptations. This is the need which the Holy Spirit promises to supply if we call on him in sincerity and are willing to give him the right of way in our lives. This is indeed the victory that overcometh the world, even our faith!

II. MISSING LIFE'S MARK

1. *The Universal Fact of Sin*

The saddest fact of human history is that "all have sinned, and come short of the glory of God" (Romans 3:23). This would be true whether the Bible revealed it or not. The whole history of the human race is a history of sin. A noted modern psychologist, having spent his life in the study of human nature, wrote two ponderous volumes entitled *The Original Nature of Man*. His conclusion, as a scientist, is that "human nature is not right, has never been right, and possibly never will be right."[1] He is but saying in modern language what David recognized long ago when he said, "Behold, I was shapen in iniquity; and in sin did my mother conceive me" (Psalm 51:5). To David's statement let us add these plain words quoted by Paul from Psalm 14: "We have before proved both Jews and Gentiles, that they are all under sin; as it is written, There is none righteous, no, not one: there is none that understandeth, there is none that seeketh after God. They are all gone out of the way, they are together become unprofitable; there is none that doeth good, no not one" (Rom. 3:9-12).

2. *What Sin Is*

There are a great many mistaken notions about the nature of sin. Some people laugh at sin, as if it were

[1] Thorndike, E. L., *The Original Nature of Man*, Vol. I, p. 281. Now out of print.

a joke. Some even try to pride themselves on their sins. There are those who lightly excuse sin as a mere fault of human nature which we cannot help. Some undertake to deny the fact of sin, speaking of it as "an error of mortal mind." Others argue that sin is a necessary part of human experience through which the race "falls upward." A New Year's party was held in a great city some time ago at which the slogan was proposed: "Bigger and better sins for the new year." A fluffy-haired young woman, after listening to a lecturer who tried to do away with sin and its punishment, came to her pastor saying, "Don't you think sin is getting better?"

Those who would trifle with sin should be led to see what God's Word has to say about it. A full hour would be all too short in which to read the Bible's terrible description and indictment of it. Here are just a few representative passages: "The heart is deceitful above all things, and desperately wicked: who can know it?" (Jer. 17:9). "But I say unto you, That whosoever looketh on a woman to lust after her hath committed adultery with her already in his heart" (Matt. 5:28). "For out of the heart proceed evil thoughts, murders, adulteries, fornications, thefts, false witness, blasphemies: These are the things which defile a man" (Matt. 15:19-20). "Whosoever committeth sin transgresseth also the law: for sin is the transgression of the law" (1 John 3:4). "All unrighteousness is sin" (1 John 5:17).

From such passages as these we build our answer to the question, What is sin? Sin is turning away from God to serve other gods. Sin is leaving the Lord out of one's heart. Sin is uncleanness of life. Sin is neglecting to keep the heart right. Sin is contamination of our human nature which has come down to us from Adam. Sin is a poison which infects the whole nature, from which come the separate acts of sin. Sin lies in the inner evil thought as well as in the outward act. Sin is the violation of God's righteous law. All unrighteousness is sin.

In the light of these truths, how can anyone think of sin other than with horror? Before we can win others from sin we must see it in its true light, as God sees it, and then lead others to turn from it in abhorrence.

3. *What Sin Does*

Ask a dozen people whom you meet on the streets, "What have you got out of sin?" The answers would no doubt surprise you. One might say, "A good time— and a headache." Another, "Acquaintances that have helped me in my business." Another, "Money that I could not have made otherwise." Still another, "Suffering and heartbreak that I did not foresee." And yet another, "Habits that have enslaved and ruined me and brought untold sorrow to those I love."

Sin is the great deceiver. It promises big wages, but the wages turn out to be *death*. One may enjoy the pleasures of sin for a season, but the season soon passes, and the so-called pleasures turn to ashes. God has not left us in the dark as to the consequences of sin. Here are some of his plain and solemn words: "And they [Adam and Eve] heard the voice of the Lord walking in the garden in the cool of the day: and Adam and his wife hid themselves from the presence of the Lord God amongst the trees of the garden" (Gen. 3:8). "And now art thou [Cain, the murderer] cursed from the earth, which hath opened her mouth to receive thy brother's blood from thy hand" (Gen. 4:11). "As righteousness tendeth to life: so that he pursueth evil pursueth it to his own death" (Prov. 11:19). "For they have sown the wind, and they shall reap the whirlwind" (Hosea 8:7). "Know ye not that the unrighteous shall not inherit the kingdom of God? Be not deceived: neither fornicators, nor idolaters, nor adulterers, nor effeminate, nor abusers of themselves with mankind, nor thieves, nor covetous, nor drunkards, nor revilers, nor extortioners, shall inherit the kingdom of God" (1 Cor. 6:9-10). "Be not deceived; God is not mocked: for whatsoever a man soweth, that shall he also reap. For he that soweth to his flesh shall of the flesh reap corruption; but he that soweth to the Spirit shall of the Spirit reap life everlasting" (Gal. 6:7-8).

What do we learn from these passages as to the consequences of sin? God's Word plainly shows us that sin brings the sense of guilt and fear, and separates us from fellowship with God. Sin brings upon the sinner the curse of hardship and suffering. Sin is not only the enemy of God but the enemy of man's soul, bringing its death. Sin takes away peace and puts trouble in its stead. Sin brings its own punishment, which cannot be escaped. Unrepented and unforgiven sin shuts the sinner out from the kingdom of God now and forever. The inexorable law is that sin brings corruption, ruin, death.

Why will not sensible men and women see this? Until we see it ourselves and then bring the lost to personal realization of the inevitable consequences of sin, we can do little toward winning them to the deliverance from sin provided in Christ.

III. THE SUPREMACY OF CHRISTIAN CHARACTER

At the opening of this chapter we reminded ourselves that the Christian claim is that Christ is sufficient for all the needs of life. The noblest thing to be said about any person is that he is Christlike. If missing life's mark is the greatest calamity that can befall us, then the supreme achievement is the attainment of Christlikeness in character—to be "sons of God."

1. *What Is Meant by Character?*

"Wash me throughly from mine iniquity, and cleanse me from my sin. . . . Create in me a clean heart, O God; and renew a right spirit within me" (Psalm 51:2, 10). "Wash you, make you clean; put away the evil of your doings from before mine eyes; cease to do evil; learn to do well; seek judgment, relieve the oppressed, judge the fatherless, plead for the widow. . . . And I will turn my hand upon thee, and purely purge away thy dross,

and take away all thy sin" (Isa. 1:16, 17, 25). "I
beseech you therefore, brethren, by the mercies of God,
that ye present your bodies a living sacrifice, holy, acceptable unto God, which is your reasonable service"
(Rom. 12:1).

Character, in the Bible, represents what a person *is*
in his or her fundamental nature. There is bad character and there is good character. A man is a good man
according as he possesses good character; he is a bad
man in proportion as his character is bad. People are
lost not because of this or that or the other particular
sin, but because they are corrupted in their original
nature and so possess character that God abhors. Jesus
came to save this lost, corrupted character with which
we are born and which needs only time to manifest itself
in outward sins. Salvation, according to the New Testament, is turning from the unrighteousness of bad character to the righteousness of good character through
Christ. It is inconceivable that a person who continues
to be fundamentally of bad character should be thought
of as saved. Salvation from sin is salvation unto righteousness.

It is not easy to define "character." Perhaps character may best be thought of as the sum total of what
a person *is* in all aspects of his life—physical, mental,
social, spiritual—as these elements gather about some
dominant purpose or purposes. Paul sets forth the ideal
of Christian character as growth toward the goal of
Christian perfection: "Till we all come in the unity of
the faith, and of the knowledge of the Son of God, unto
a perfect man, unto the measure of the stature of the
fulness of Christ: that we henceforth be no more children, tossed to and fro, and carried about with every
wind of doctrine, by the sleight of men, and cunning
craftiness, whereby they lie in wait to deceive; but
speaking the truth in love, may grow up into him in
all things, which is the head, even Christ" (Eph. 4:13-
15).

2. *Why Is Christian Character Supremely Important?*

"Know ye not that the unrighteous shall not inherit the kingdom of God? Be not deceived: neither fornicators, nor idolaters, nor adulterers, nor effeminate, nor abusers of themselves with mankind, nor thieves, nor covetous, nor drunkards, nor revilers, nor extortioners, shall inherit the kingdom of God" (1 Cor. 6:9-10).

The greatest need in human life today is for genuine Christian character. Here are some evidences worthy of study.

"One of America's best known businessmen was recently asked this question, 'What do you consider the most important single quality or characteristic essential to a man's success?' He answered instantly, 'Integrity.' Then he continued, 'I can buy all of the technical skill, ability, or knowledge that I want for five or six thousand dollars a year; but I'll gladly pay several times this amount for the same skill, ability, or knowledge combined with integrity.' *'Integrity'* is a simple sounding term, until it is analyzed into its multitude of important elements such as honesty, truthfulness, fairness, co-operation, and reliability, and appreciated as the evidence of all civil virtues.

"Coolidge evaluated character in these words, 'It is not only what men know, but what they are disposed to do with what they know that will determine the rise and fall of civilization.' Later, Herbert Hoover stated in similar vein, 'Social values outrank economic values. Economic gains, even scientific gains, are worse than useless if they accrue to a people unfitted by trained character to use, and not abuse them.' "[2]

If character is put first in the ordinary business, political, and social relationships of life, do we not see clearly that it must be put first in the lives of Christians? It is absurd to think that the unconverted people of the world can be influenced for Christ by professing church members whose character does not even come up to the

_____
[2]McKown, H. C., *Character Education*, pp. 6, 7.

standard set by unsaved business and professional people.

3. *How Is Christian Character Achieved?*

"For this cause I bow my knees unto the Father of our Lord Jesus Christ, of whom the whole family in heaven and earth is named, That he would grant you, according to the riches of his glory, to be strengthened with might by his Spirit in the inner man; that Christ may dwell in your hearts by faith; that ye, being rooted and grounded in love, may be able to comprehend with all saints what is the breadth, and length, and depth, and height; and to know the love of Christ, which passeth knowledge, that ye might be filled with all the fulness of God" (Eph. 3:14-19).

Character is basically a matter of *being*. In this great prayer of Paul's, he prays for the Ephesians that they may *be*, not that they may *have*. He prays that they may be strengthened in the inner man, that Christ may dwell in their hearts by faith, that they may be able to know the love of Christ, that they may be filled with the fulness of God. Paul is praying for Christians who are already saved, but who must grow in knowledge and in grace through the power of the Holy Spirit leading them on to new levels of sanctification. It is clear that the fulness of Christian character does not come at the moment of conversion, but that it is a never-ending process of Christian growth from stage to stage. Christian character is therefore the product of a process. We must never forget that we have our part in the building of Christlike personality, and that we hinder the Holy Spirit from doing his part unless we do ours. He who would win others to Christ must himself experience continuous growth in Christlikeness.

4. *Why Is Christian Character Contagious?*

Emerson has an oft-quoted statement: "What you are stands over you . . . and thunders so that I cannot hear what you say." The most powerful witness that any of us bears is the witness of the life we live. We say of one man, "He has a good influence." We say of another, "He has a bad influence." When we speak thus we are not usually thinking so much about what each man says as what he is. "Influence" is that indefinable something that flows out of one life into the lives of others. This influence may be for good or evil, it may be for Christ or against Christ. No man is all good, and no man is all bad, but when the total impact of any man's life is summed up, it will be found to have been either for or against Jesus Christ. This is what Jesus meant when he said, "He that is not with me is against me."

The simple truth is that we are all bound up in the same bundle of humanity, wherein no man lives to himself and no man dies to himself. It is a terrifying thought to realize that one's life may be a source of infection, through evil influence, that will cause others to go deep into sin and fail to turn from it, resulting in their eternal death.

"There is a subtle, intangible, but very real spirit influence breathing out of every man's presence. It is proportioned entirely to the strength of the man living within. With some it is very attractive. Sometimes it is positively repulsive. It is the expression of the man within. The presence becomes the mould of the spirit within, large or small, noble or mean, coarse or fine, as he makes it. The strength of a man's will or its weakness; the purity of his heart or its lack of purity; the ideals of his life, high or low; the keenness or slowness of his thinking—all these express themselves in his presence.

"Now this is the chief thing we have for our winning work. This is the thing that Jesus uses. It is this that the Spirit of God takes possession of, if he may, and that he uses in his outreach to others. We win most and best through what we are."[3]

---

[3]Gordon, S. D., *Quiet Talks with World Winners*, p. 181.

QUESTIONS FOR REVIEW AND CLASS DISCUSSION

1. In its broadest sense, what is *evangelism?* What are some inadequate forms of evangelism? What kind of evangelism do we most need today?

2. Why do we especially need spiritual wisdom? What is the source of this needed wisdom?

3. What are some of the chief difficulties in the way of spiritual living in our day? How should we as Christians face the problems of life that threaten sometimes to overwhelm us?

4. What temptations especially beset us today? What is our hope of overcoming these temptations?

5. What do the Scriptures and modern psychology say as to the extent of sin? What is the essential nature of sin? How must the Christian feel about sin?

6. What are the terrible consequences of sin? What certain punishment does sin bring?

7. What are the effects of sin on character? What is the Christian ideal of character? How is this ideal to be achieved?

8. What value is placed by the world on good character? Why is Christian character supremely important?

9. When one becomes a Christian, does he instantly attain to perfection of character? How is Christian character achieved?

10. Why is sound Christian character of utmost importance in soul-winning? What is the source of our power and influence in winning others to Christ?

THE SUPREME TASK

OUTLINE

I. THE LESSONS OF PENTECOST
  1. The Lesson of Preparedness
  2. The Lesson of Every-Member Witnessing
  3. The Lesson of Rich Harvesting

II. THE PASSION AND PRACTICE OF PAUL
  1. Paul's Sensitiveness to Spiritual Guidance
  2. Paul's Courage and Compassion
  3. Paul's Skill in Winning the Lost

III. THE CHURCH'S COMMISSION TO WITNESS
  1. The Sublime Simplicity of Christ's Plan
  2. What It Means to "Witness"
  3. Who Ought to Do the Witnessing?
  4. How a Church Can Best Witness
  5. To Whom We Shall Bear Witness

IV. THE MARKS OF A SOUL-WINNING CHURCH
  1. A Church of Real Christians
  2. A Church with a Warm-Hearted Welcome
  3. A Church with Passionate Concern for the Unsaved
  4. A Church That Continually Seeks the Lost

THE SUPREME TASK

The supreme task of the church was set by the Founder of the church—the greatest soul-winner of all time. How to win others by means of the "gospel," the "good news," is the practice we may learn from Jesus himself. Out of that practice has been built the doctrine of evangelism as the crowning purpose of the church.

When we turn to study the methods of the Master Evangelist we do not find him primarily winning men to join his church. Rather we find him winning men to an abundant and eternal life which then found expression in church fellowship and service. The appeal of Jesus was always life-centered. There was nothing mechanical about his method in dealing with men and women. He loved people, and was filled with a consuming passion for those whom sin had undone. He began with people where they were, simply and naturally, and led them to self-revelation, a sense of need, and decision based on free choice.

Jesus went at once to the root of the matter, *sin*, and refused to be sidetracked by minor matters. He demanded uncompromisingly a turning from sin and a turning to God through faith in himself. He dealt with the great issues of life and death, yet his profoundest utterances were in simple, understandable language.

Jesus wept over the unsaved multitudes, but he dealt with them not in crowds but as individuals. He was patient in making clear the conditions of salvation, but urgent in pressing for decision on the part of one who understood his meaning. He depended implicitly upon his Father, God, never undertaking anything without prayer. He imparted his compassion, his enthusiasm, his love, his redeeming message to his followers, sending them out to tell others, and they others, and they others, in ever-widening circles until some day all people everywhere shall know of his salvation.

Imbued with these principles, the first Christians went forth to put them into practice. From the Master and his disciples we can best learn the way to make our witness effectual.

I. THE LESSONS OF PENTECOST

1. *The Lesson of Preparedness*

Pentecost illustrates the evangelistic program of Christ in action. Of the more than five hundred who met him by appointment just before his ascension, one hundred and twenty were gripped by a great faith. They had been trained in the school of Christ, some of them throughout his ministry. They knew his mind, his message, his methods. Doubtless they were eager to begin. But they had learned the lesson of obedience, and he had commanded them to wait until promised power came.

This period of waiting was not idly spent. Gathered in an upper room in Jerusalem, they held a ten-day prayer meeting, the like of which the world perhaps never knew before nor since. These men and women were on fire to share their experiences, to tell the story of Christ's resurrection, to proclaim the marvelous message which he had given them. Then when prayer had done its perfect work the power fell—the irresistible power of the Holy Spirit. God was ready all along, but they were not, until prayer prepared them, even though they had spent three years with Jesus; and when the final preparation was completed their witness became invincible.

Have we any right to expect an outpouring of the Holy Spirit upon us unless we are prepared to receive him? Pentecost was the climax of more than three years of preparation, in which the disciples had walked and talked with Jesus, and had come to be identified with him in spirit and in purpose. The supremely important matter was their closeness to Jesus, their implicit obedience, their hearts filled with love for him and for the lost. Could not any church have a pentecostal revival that was willing to pay the price of these simple requirements?

2. *The Lesson of Every-Member Witnessing*

Notice that the first work of the disciples was not preaching, but every-member witnessing. Men and women mingled with the mob of curiosity-seekers, and gathering about them people who spoke the same language told the story of Jesus, no doubt asking and answering questions. Remember that these were Jews or Jewish proselytes, many of whom had known Jesus in the flesh, all of whom had been stirred by the events of his death and resurrection, and all of whom knew the Jewish or Old Testament Scriptures. They were ripe for his witness, and through it the way was prepared for the marvelous results that followed.

Have we not often made a mistake at this point? The crowd came together at Pentecost, and was then divided into smaller groups, into the midst of which the disciples, men and women, went to do personal work. Can you not, in your imagination, see these spirit-filled men and women as they stood in the midst of these smaller groups, telling the story of Jesus, answering questions and objections, explaining what was not clearly understood, until they had laid a background of knowledge for the preaching service that was to follow? Suppose one hundred twenty people of any church, thus filled with the Holy Spirit, should go forth to bear personal witness and do personal work several hours before the preaching of the evangelistic sermon at the church. Can anyone doubt the results?

3. *The Lesson of Rich Harvesting*

Jesus, in his last discourse with his disciples before his crucifixion, said to them, "Ye have not chosen me, but I have chosen you, and ordained you, that ye should go and bring forth fruit, and that your fruit should remain: that whatsoever ye shall ask of the Father in my name, he may give it you" (John 15:16). Jesus has called us to be winners, not failures. He expected great things of these first disciples, and they attempted great things for him.

The witness of his fellow disciples had prepared the minds of the multitude for Peter's soul-stirring sermon. The preacher did not dismiss the crowd, saying, "Go home now, and think this over, and come to hear me preach again." Instead, Peter pressed for immediate decision. The people, pricked to the heart, unable longer to keep silence, cried, "What shall we do?" Whereupon the preacher, having made his case, applied the gospel remedy: "Repent, and be baptized every one of you in the name of Jesus Christ for the remission of sins." "The promise," he declared, "is unto you, and to your children, and to all that are afar off, even as many as the Lord our God shall call." Reinforced by the presence and help of the other disciples, Peter continued to press the invitation as he testified and exhorted, saying, "Save yourselves from this untoward generation." (See Acts 2:38-40.)

What was the outcome of this first day's Spirit-filled witnessing? "Then they that gladly received his word were baptized: and the same day there were added unto them about three thousand souls" (Acts 2:41).

What object has a church for existence if it is not in the business of winning souls? True, there are many activities in a church, but is there anything which a church ought to do that does not lead toward winning the lost? This is not the occasional business of a church, but its everyday business twelve months in a year. Suppose the more than twenty-four thousand Southern Baptist churches would take this model given by the Holy Spirit at Pentecost and seek earnestly and zealously to reproduce its values. The greatest revival of modern times would result! Shall we not say, "As for our church, we will this very year undertake it"?

II. The Passion and Practice of Paul

1. *Paul's Sensitiveness to Spiritual Guidance*

At Paul's conversion, God became to him a present spiritual reality. Christ was no faraway being, but a living Lord who dwelt in his heart by faith. The Holy Spirit was not just a name and an influence, but a personal teacher and guide available for every need. Paul had a great mind, but he did not depend upon his own reasoning ability. He put his mind completely at the disposal of Christ, and subjected his every power to the leadership of the Holy Spirit. This spiritual sensitiveness did for him two things—it kept him from mistakes which he might otherwise have made, and it gave him a positiveness and assurance that guaranteed him against failure.

Paul's spiritual sensitiveness is revealed in scores of instances. He tells us that when he was converted he "conferred not with flesh and blood," but withdrew to Arabia, where he spent three years thinking through his experience and the claims of Christ, and getting ready for his life work. When the Holy Spirit spoke to the church at Antioch, saying, "Separate me Barnabas and Saul for the work whereunto I have called them" (Acts 13:2), unhesitatingly Paul accepted the call and set out on his first missionary journey. Later, when Paul stood at attention not knowing what to do, the Holy Spirit having closed the doors eastward, Paul heard the Holy Spirit's call through the man of Macedonia and forthwith crossed over to the western continent. When his friends pleaded with him not to go to Jerusalem, having been warned of the danger involved, Paul answered, "What mean ye to weep and to break mine heart? for I am ready not to be bound only, but also to die at Jerusalem for the name of the Lord Jesus" (Acts 21:13).

Why should we doubt Christ's promise of the Holy Spirit's guidance? We are to use all the sense and judgment we have in our work for Christ, but if we will put our reason at the disposal of the Holy Spirit he will illuminate our thinking, give poise to our judgment, direct our decisions, thus saving us from mistakes and preventing our failure. Can any Christian have the Holy Spirit's guidance? Yes; provided he is willing to meet the conditions. How vastly more successful would be our work for Christ if, like Paul, we cultivated and maintained this spiritual sensitiveness!

2. Paul's Courage and Compassion

Paul was no coward. He did mighty things for Christ, yet there was in him no pride, no hint of boastfulness. "God forbid," he disclaimed, "that I should glory, save in the cross of our Lord Jesus Christ, by whom the world is crucified unto me, and I unto the world" (Gal. 6:14). Having been crucified with Christ, all fear of death left him. He was like the young missionary to whom someone said, as he was getting ready to leave for Africa, "Aren't you afraid you'll die out there?" "Why, no," the missionary quietly replied, "I died when I decided to go."

Paul loved people. When he fell in love with Christ he fell in love with all those for whom Christ had died. Paul saw through the eyes of his Master that every soul is infinitely precious, and has in it unlimited possibilities. His heart went out in deep compassion to the needy, the sick, the suffering, the ignorant, the deluded, the despised, the sin-enslaved. He bore witness with equal fervor to the ignorant barbarians and to the learned Greeks. On occasion he boldly denounced sin, but before he finished there was always the note of tender pleading. His heart went out in passionate concern for those who were missing the meaning of life and making shipwreck of their souls. Listen to these compassionate words from his great heart: "I say the truth in Christ, I lie not, my conscience also bearing me witness in the Holy Ghost, that I have great heaviness and continual sorrow in my heart. For I could wish that myself were accursed from Christ for my brethren, my kinsmen according to the flesh (Rom. 9:1-3). Can we hope to win for Christ until our hearts, too, have been thus touched for those who are lost?

3. *Paul's Skill in Winning the Lost*

The secret of Paul's success as a soul-winner may be found in his own words: "For though I be free from all men, yet have I made myself servant unto all, that I might gain the more. And unto the Jews I became as a Jew, that I might gain the Jews; to them that are under the law, as under the law, that I might gain them that are under the law, to them that are without law, as without law, (being not without law to God, but under the law to Christ), that I might gain them that are without law. To the weak became I as weak, that I might gain the weak: I am made all things to all men, that I might by all means save some" (1 Cor. 9:19-22).

Summed up, we find his superb skill in winning others demonstrated in these points:

(1) He began with the lost on their own level.

(2) He won their confidence and esteem.

(3) He dealt frankly and honestly with sin.

(4) He held up the crucified Christ as the only Saviour.

(5) He demanded true repentance and faith as the only conditions of salvation.

(6) He pressed earnestly and boldly for immediate decision, confession, and baptism.

(7) He refused to be discouraged, never giving up, no matter how great the difficulties, and rejoicing in every indication of success.

(8) He carefully organized and taught those who were converted to the end that they might go out and win others.

What better outline could we ask for a soul-winning program, both for ourselves as individuals and for our churches?

III. The Church's Commission to Witness

Every enterprise must be finally judged by its product. A farm is judged by the crops it produces; a factory is judged by the goods it turns out; a school is judged by its graduates; and a church must be judged by the souls it has won to Christ and enlisted in his service. It is easy to confuse *ends* with *means*. A church may make use of many *means*—building equipment, instruction, music, worship, giving, service, fellowship. But what is the great *end* toward which these means should always move? What is it that Christ has commissioned his church to do, above all else?

1. *The Sublime Simplicity of Christ's Plan*

Just before he ascended to the Father, Jesus gathered about him his disciples and said to them, "All power is given unto me in heaven and in earth. Go ye therefore, and teach all nations, baptizing them in the name of the Father, and of the Son, and of the Holy Ghost: teaching them to observe all things whatsoever I have commanded you: and, lo, I am with you alway, even unto the end of the world. Amen" (Matt. 28:19-20).

Stop for a moment to consider how sublimely simple is Christ's plan. Those who have had a personal experience with him, and have learned to love and trust him, are to go out and tell others what he has done for them and persuade them, too, to turn from sin and self to the redeeming Saviour. They who yield themselves to Christ as Saviour and Lord, and receive from him power to become children of God, go forth with zeal and enthusiasm to find others whom they bring to their Saviour. These then go out and find yet others whom they bring into the circle. Thus redeemed by the grace of God in Christ, they bind themselves into churches, or organized bodies of baptized believers, in order that they may bear more effective witness united together than they could as separate individuals.

If every true church of Jesus Christ in the world should enlist all its truly saved members in this supreme business of finding and winning others, beginning where they are and extending their witness unto the uttermost part of the earth, the gospel message could be brought with power to nearly every one of the two billions of souls in the world within this generation.

Is a church true to its commission that goes a whole year without having won at least one soul to the Saviour?

2. What It Means to "Witness"

The word "witness" is a legal term. It is taken from court procedure, a *witness* being one who, in a trial at law, possesses certain evidence which he is called upon to relate. When Jesus said that we are to be his "witnesses," what did he mean?

A good witness is one who offers facts, not hearsay evidence. The witness must know by experience that to which he testifies. He must be of good character in order for his testimony to bear weight. He must tell the truth, and nothing but the truth. The simpler and more direct and sincere his testimony, the more impressive it will be. Are not these fundamental qualifications of the Christian witness?

Let us imagine a court trial. The questions at issue are: Who is Jesus Christ? Is he the divine Son of God? Can he save unto the uttermost all who come to God through him? An unbelieving world, under the power of Satan, answers "No!" Those who know whereof they speak because they have experienced Christ's divine power and have been saved by him whom they trust and love, are summoned to take the stand. Jesus Christ says to those who believe on him and have been saved by him: "Ye shall be witnesses unto me both in Jerusalem [your home community], and in all Judea [your state], and in Samaria [the outlying regions], and unto the uttermost part of the earth [the foreign fields]" (Acts 1:8).

The questions which confront us are, What sort of witnesses are we? Are we the sort of witnesses who slip out of court in order to escape bearing testimony? Are we the sort of witnesses who, at the crucial moment, are discovered to have nothing worth while to tell? Are we the sort of witnesses whose testimony wavers and contradicts itself? Or are we the sort of witnesses who know what we have to say, and who tell it with straightforwardness and convincing power? How many are there who rarely, if ever, open their mouths in testimony for the Saviour? A church can never be the sort of church it should be until every member is a living and active witness, testifying daily, by his life and his lips, to the validity of the claims of Jesus and to the reality of his saving power.

3. *Who Ought to Do the Witnessing?*

Jesus said, "Go *ye* therefore," "*ye* shall be witnesses unto me." Evidently he meant that every Christian, without exception, should be a witness to the saving power of the living Christ. The minister, of course, is expected to lead the way and set the example. Every deacon and every church officer should realize that this is his first responsibility. Sunday school officers and teachers are under peculiar obligation to be Christ's witnesses. Leaders of the Training Union must put this business of daily witnessing above every other duty. Indeed, every person who has been given any office in the church is declared thereby to be a Christian witness, and if unfaithful at this point is a relative failure, no matter what else he may do.

But the duty of Christian witnessing extends beyond the "inner circle" of officers and leaders of the church to every member. Not all can preach or teach or serve in official capacity, but there is no Christian who loves Christ who cannot speak a good word for him to another, or who cannot by conduct and influence help turn another to the Saviour. Is it not glorious to realize that the most important thing our Lord has commanded us to do is that which any Christian can do?

4. *How a Church Can Best Witness*

There are three main ways in which a church can best fulfil its commission to witness for Jesus Christ. One way, and the chief way, is in teaching and inspiring its members to be personal witnesses. The greatest single service that any church can render to Christ is in getting all its members ready and willing to be good witnesses for him among their friends and acquaintances, at home and in their places of business, in everyday contacts and relationships.

The second way in which a church can bear most effectual witness is by bringing together the unsaved in the teaching and preaching services of the church. Teaching and preaching have been divinely ordained as means by which the unsaved are to be taught the saving truth of the gospel and won to an acceptance of the Saviour. There can be no substitute for a church in which the gospel is taught and preached in the Holy Spirit's power. Clearly, however, preaching and teaching cannot reach those who are not present. Are we bringing the lost to our Sunday school classes and into the preaching services?

The third way we may bear effectual witness as a church is in the gift of our money to send others where we cannot go. The range of any church's direct influence is limited. If we are to go into all the world and preach the gospel to every creature we must do so through our missionary representatives. Missions is evangelism that has gone from Jerusalem and Judea and Samaria unto the uttermost parts of the earth. A church cannot be fully true to its commission until every member is having some share in sending the whole gospel to the whole world.

5. *To Whom We Shall Bear Witness*

To whom shall we bear our witness? Let us make a list of those for whom Christ has made us responsible:

(1) The unsaved members of our own households.

(2) Unsaved acquaintances and neighbors who live about us and with whom we have daily contacts.

(3) Servants in the home, and those who serve us in the many capacities of modern business life.

(4) Strangers whom we meet in various ways, whom we can tactfully invite to Sunday school, Training Union, and church and whom we can engage in conversation about spiritual things.

(5) Unsaved members of our Sunday school classes and others who are attached in some way to the church and its ministries.

(6) Those who live beyond our immediate contact, who may be in hospitals, jails, orphanages, or other institutions, but whom we may visit and bear Christ's message of love.

(7) Those whose faces we may never see, but to whom we can send the gospel message by means of our missionary representatives.

How worldwide is the circle of those to whom we may bear witness! And how glorious is the privilege to begin in our own homes and extend our witness until it reaches unto the ends of the earth!

IV. THE MARKS OF A SOUL-WINNING CHURCH

1. *A Church of Real Christians*

What is a church? It is a body of baptized believers organized to carry out Christ's Great Commission. A true church is the body of Jesus Christ, and those who belong to it are members severally thereof.

A soul-winning church begins first with its own members. It seeks to feed and nurture and exercise them so that they may grow in grace and in the knowledge of the Lord Jesus Christ. The unconverted will not see Christ when cold, worldly, selfish lives of church members stand between him and them. Religion is a deeply personal matter. The unconverted person says, "Mrs.

Blank is a real Christian. I wish I were like her."
Or the unconverted person may say, "If being a Christian
is to be like Mr. Blank, excuse me." It is easier for
people to love and trust Jesus Christ if they have confidence in those who claim to be his representatives; and
it is exceedingly difficult for our Lord to reach the lost
with his saving power if the inconsistent lives of his
church members get in the way. The greatest single
responsibility of any church is to develop its members
"unto the measure of the stature of the fulness of
Christ." A church made up of Christlike Christians is
bound to be a soul-winning church.

2. *A Church with a Warm-Hearted Welcome*

It is a pity when a church gets the reputation of being
cold and unfriendly. A church defeats the very purpose
for which it exists when the sinful, the down-and-out,
the lonely, the grieved and troubled, the heartsick and
weary feel that they are not wanted in its services and
that it has no message for them. A church of Jesus
Christ should not be a church of any special class. In
the house of God the rich and the poor sit down together,
assured that the Lord is the Maker of them all. (Read
James 2: 1-5.)

Not only in the public services of worship but also in
the daily contacts of its members, a church that would
win must show its interest in people. Its members must
visit in the homes of strangers, bring sympathy to those
who are sick and in sorrow, help those who are in trouble
and in need, ministering always in the Spirit of Jesus
Christ to high and low alike. A church with this spirit
of warm friendliness will open the door for Jesus Christ
to come into many hearts that otherwise would be closed.

Are we cultivating as we ought this spirit of friendliness in our churches? Do we make strangers welcome,
introducing ourselves to them and then introducing them
to others? Do we follow up their visit to the churches
with visits to them in their homes? Are we always on

the lookout for opportunities for friendliness and service in the name of Jesus Christ? Measured by their spirit of genuine friendliness, how do our churches rate?

3. *A Church with Passionate Concern for the Unsaved*

It is easy to grow indifferent toward the lost multitudes around us. A veteran pastor of a great church, realizing that he had gone a year and more without anybody being saved, called his deacons together. He proposed to resign unless this condition could be changed. The deacons protested, saying that they were getting along very well, and that everybody was enjoying his preaching. Turning to these men in great earnestness, the pastor repeated his determination to resign the pastorate of the church unless souls were saved within the next month. He then questioned the deacons one by one as to whether they had ever been instrumental in the salvation of a soul. One after another confessed that, so far as he knew, he had never won a soul to Christ. The pastor then made this proposal: that unless God gave the church souls in the near future, both pastor and deacons would resign.

Finally, the pastor relates, they all knelt down and prayed together, and in that prayer a covenant was made that they would resign if the Lord did not give souls in the near future. They went to their homes; it was Saturday night.

Monday morning the deacon questioned by the pastor went into his store. The first man he met was his confidential clerk. He took him into his office, shut the door behind him, and after earnest conversation and prayer, led him to Christ.

The deacon called in another, and another, and another, and in that one day he led eleven men to Christ. The next Sunday over thirty men were received into that church upon profession of faith; every one of them led to Jesus Christ by an official in the church who had up to that time never had part in the saving of a soul.

Suppose deacons, church officers, Sunday school officers and teachers, Training Union, Woman's Missionary Union, and Brotherhood leaders, were called together and the proposition made that they covenant together with the pastor not to let another month pass without each one making an honest and earnest effort to win someone to the Saviour. How glorious would be the results! Measured by this test of every-member witnessing, how strong are our churches?

4. A Church That Continually Seeks the Lost

We read concerning that first great church in Jerusalem, which had the guidance of the Holy Spirit in such remarkable measure, that they "continuing daily with one accord in the temple, and breaking bread from house to house, did eat their meat with gladness and singleness of heart, praising God, and having favour with all the people. And the Lord added to the church daily such as should be saved" (Acts 2: 46-47). Notice the repeated word "daily."

This great Jerusalem church did not wait until the last two weeks in August to go out on its quest for souls. Nor did difficulty and persecutions prevent their witness, for we read that "they that were scattered abroad went everywhere preaching the word." They did not wait until a preacher came from a distance to hold a meeting for them, but every Christian became a preacher, a proclaimer of the good news of salvation in Christ, a winner of souls. Put together these words "daily" "every one," "everywhere," and you have the New Testament ideal of evangelism. Is it not strange that we Baptists who make so much of our devotion to the New Testament as our sole and sufficient guide, should have got so far away from it in this fundamental matter?

To what extent are we pleasing the Holy Spirit and honoring Christ by a program of continuous soul-winning?

QUESTIONS FOR REVIEW AND CLASS DISCUSSION

1. Recall several examples of Jesus' work as soul-winner—the first two disciples, Nicodemus, the woman at the well, the blind beggar, Matthew, Zaccheus, and others. Give five principles of soul-winning that are illustrated in the practice of Jesus.

2. What three main lessons concerning evangelism do we learn from a study of Pentecost?

3. Consider the evangelistic program of your church. At what points is it similar to the procedures followed at Pentecost? At what points does it differ?

4. In Christ's plan, who are to do the witnessing? How account for the fact that so few members of a typical Baptist church are soul-winners?

5. What do you consider the chief reasons for Paul's success as an evangelist?

6. State the four principal marks of a soul-winning church. If twenty-five points were allowed for each of these essentials, how high on the scale of 100 points would your church rate? What does this indicate as to its weakest points?

7. What are the three main ways in which a church can best fulfil its commission to witness? In what ways do you feel that you can best do your part?

8. Give several ways by which a church can attract the unsaved to its preaching and teaching services.

9. Which is more important in successful evangelism, preaching or personal work? Why should they always go together?

10. Why should every church have a continuous as well as an occasional program of evangelism?

A FULL SALVATION

OUTLINE

I. SALVATION BY GRACE THROUGH FAITH UNTO GOOD WORKS
1. Salvation
2. Salvation by Grace
3. Salvation Through Faith
4. Salvation unto Good Works

II. THE NECESSITY OF PUBLIC CONFESSION
1. God Requires Confession of Sin
2. Baptism, a Pictured Confession
3. Jesus Plainly Commands Public Confession
4. Confession, an Evidence of Salvation

III. COMMITTAL TO THE CHRISTIAN IDEAL
1. The Ideal of Repentance
2. The Ideal of Faith
3. The Ideal of Obedience
4. The Ideal of Unselfishness
5. The Ideal of Service

A FULL SALVATION

It is a tragic fact that the majority of the people in the world do not know how to be saved. We need to keep our thinking clear on a subject of such vital importance as this, both for our own sake, and for the sake of those who need our help.

I. SALVATION BY GRACE THROUGH FAITH UNTO GOOD WORKS

1. *Salvation*

There are some words in our language too great for definition. Such a word is "salvation." It means that what was in danger has been made safe; that what was about to be ruined is restored; that what was lost is found; that what was worthless has been given value.

The most precious thing in this universe is a human soul. The soul was made for an eternal life with God. Yet because of sin the soul is separated from God, lost and ruined, and made fit for nothing except an eternity of hell. Could anything in all the universe be more tragic, that the most precious thing God ever made should be forever separated from him, that the most priceless of all God's creation should be lost and ruined? What could be more awful to contemplate than an immortal soul, made to live forever with God, dragged by sin from God's presence into an eternity of suffering and remorse?

How can a soul be freed from this terrible guilt of sin? Perhaps someone will say, "By never committing sin." But this holds out no hope, for all have sinned. Perhaps someone else will say, "By doing more good than evil." But both the Bible and common sense tell us that "by the works of the law shall no flesh be justified" (Gal. 2: 16). Salvation must do more than prevent us from ever committing sin or give us standing before God because of our own righteousness. Salvation must come to us in our sins, pay the penalty of the broken law, and break the power of sin over our lives. Salvation, if it is to be what the word means, must give us a new standing with God, provide a new nature, instil a new motive, and furnish power from above to live a new life.

It is such a complete and absolute salvation that Paul declares he has found in Christ: "For I through the law am dead to the law, that I might live unto God. I am crucified with Christ: nevertheless I live; yet not I, but Christ liveth in me: and the life which I now live in the flesh I live by the faith of the Son of God, who loved me, and gave himself for me" (Gal. 2: 19, 20).

2. *Salvation by Grace*

The great mistake of the Jews was that they thought they could somehow earn salvation. The good news which Christ came to bring was that salvation does not depend in any wise upon forms, ceremonies, good works, self-righteousness. Paul had preached this simple gospel to the Galatians, and many had accepted it. Then there had come false teachers who declared that it was necessary to be circumcised, and to keep the law of Moses, in order to be saved. Paul assails this false teaching with trip-hammer blows. "O foolish Galatians, who hath bewitched you, that ye should not obey the truth, before whose eyes Jesus Christ hath been evidently set forth, crucified among you?" (Gal. 3: 1.) He rebukes them for having fallen away from this great principle of salvation by grace and of having gone back to the old dead principle of salvation by works. Do they argue that they must be children of Abraham in order to be saved? Even so, Paul declares, the true children of Abraham are those who have accepted Christ by faith. "So then they which be of faith are blessed with faithful Abraham" (Gal. 3: 9).

Salvation must be all of works or all of grace. There can be no middle ground. There is but one possible way by which salvation could be merited, and that is by living a perfectly sinless life from the moment of birth to the moment of death. But our conscience and experience declare this impossible, since we all commit sin as soon as we reach the age of accountability. We conclude, therefore, that we are saved by grace alone, "And if by grace, then is it no more of works: otherwise grace is no more grace. But if it be of works, then is it no more grace: otherwise work is no more work" (Rom. 11: 6).

3. *Salvation Through Faith*

The trouble with trying to deserve salvation is that one must keep the law perfectly at every point during the whole of life. Moses clearly wrote, "Cursed is every one that continueth not in all things which are written in the book of the law to do them." Since none of us can meet this requirement, it follows that "as many as are of the works of the law are under the curse" (Gal. 3: 10). Human nature being what it is, and sin being what it is, what hope is there that any man should be justified by the law in the sight of God? If anybody is to be saved, therefore, it must be according to a new principle. This new principle is that of salvation given freely by God's grace and accepted humbly by man's faith. Thus we come to that great word through which Martin Luther shook the foundations of Roman Catholicism during the days of the Reformation, "The just shall live by faith!"

How does faith help to save? It is somewhat as if a man were in a deep pit from which he could not escape and in which he must die if he is not rescued. Someone lowers a rope to him and says, "Catch hold of the rope and we will pull you up to safety!" But if the man is afraid that the rope will break, or if he is unwilling to trust the one who proposes to pull him up, and so will not catch hold of the rope, he will not be saved from the death which threatens. If God were to save the lost man against his will it would not be true salvation, because salvation implies a new relation to God, an active faith in Christ, a changed way of believing and behaving. Salvation does more than rescue the sinner from hell; it makes a new man of him, gives him a new standing with God, puts a new motive in his heart and a new song on his lips. Christ takes the sinner's place, so that the condemned sinner now goes free. Paul therefore thus concludes: "Christ hath redeemed us from the curse of the law, being made a curse for us: for it is written, Cursed is every one that hangeth on a tree" (Gal. 3: 13).

4. Salvation unto Good Works

What then becomes of the moral law? Are the Ten Commandments done away with? Does it make any difference how the Christian lives, since he is saved by grace? Paul immediately deals with such questions as these. "Is the law then against the promises of God? God forbid: for if there had been a law given which could have given life, verily righteousness should have been by the law" (Gal. 3: 21). Right has always been right, and wrong has always been wrong. Christ did not come to destroy but to fulfil the law.

Salvation is *from* something *to* something. To say that one could be saved and yet left to live in his sins is like saying that one could be rescued from drowning and still left in the water, or rescued from fire and still left in the flames. To be saved one must be rescued *from* danger *to* safety. It is so with the Christian's salvation —he is saved *from* sin *to* righteousness, *from* evil works *to* good works.

The figure which Paul uses in Galatians 3: 22-23 is that of a great walled city of sin and death, with all its inhabitants doomed. Then a door is revealed, and all are urged to come out of the city of death into the life that awaits them outside. Many will not heed the invitation, and so die. But some have faith to come out, and when these are delivered by their Guide they discover a new life of safety and joy and fruitfulness.

Let us never forget that the Christian is saved unto good works. He is not saved *by* good works, but if there are no good works it is an indication that he has not been saved. To say that one has experienced salvation whose nature and conduct remain the same and who does not produce the fruits of a saved life would be to use words that contradict one another. To be saved in this true Christian sense means that we have become "the children of God by faith in Christ Jesus" (Gal. 3: 26).

II. THE NECESSITY OF PUBLIC CONFESSION

Have you not heard people say, "Yes, I think I am a Christian; I believe in Jesus Christ, and I am trusting him for salvation, but I have never been baptized and have not joined a church"? Pressed for reasons as to why they have thus been disobedient to Christ's plain command, they reply variously. Perhaps one will admit that he has just put it off. Perhaps another will argue that baptism and church membership are not essential to salvation, therefore he feels as well off as if he had become a member of the church. Still another may argue that there are so many "hypocrites" in the church that he feels better off on the outside than on the inside. How shall we meet these excuses and objections? How shall we convince such people of the necessity of public confession? Let us turn to the Scriptures for our reply.

1. *God Requires Confession of Sin*

From Adam until now people have sinned. When we sin, what are we to do about it? We cannot escape God's knowledge of our sin. We cannot rid ourselves of our sin by our own power. No human agency or ceremony can wash our sin away. The fact keeps staring us in the face: we have sinned. What can we do about it?

Confess it! Don't deny it, don't try to hide it, don't excuse it, just acknowledge it to God! This is something that we can do, and it is the best thing to do. Over and over God commands us to confess our sins, and promises forgiveness on the basis of confession.

When Solomon had completed the building of the Temple he assembled the elders and all the men of Israel in a great service of dedication. As a part of this dedication service, Solomon called on the people to enter into a covenant. God spoke through Solomon to the people, telling them what to do when smitten before the enemy and defeated because of their sins. Solomon pleads with God on behalf of the people that "if they pray toward this place, and confess thy name, and turn from their sin, when thou dost afflict them; then hear thou from heaven, and forgive the sin of thy servants, and of thy people Israel" (2 Chron. 6: 26, 27). It is clear that God's approval and blessing and forgiveness depend upon sincere confession. Need we hope for God's smile upon us if we go stubbornly ahead with unconfessed sin in our lives and hearts?

2. *Baptism, a Pictured Confession*

John the Baptist came preaching, "Repent ye: for the kingdom of heaven is at hand" (Matt. 3: 2). It was not enough for men to agree with him that they ought to repent. He called upon them to take a stand, to declare themselves, to get on the side of those who received his message and were willing to get ready for the coming Saviour. As evidence of the reality of their changed minds and hearts, John called upon them to submit themselves to a meaningful and eloquent ceremony. They were to go down into the water, signifying their death to the old life. They were to be buried beneath the water, symbolizing that the old life had been completely buried. Then they were to come up out of the water to walk in a new life—a life committed to righteousness and to the service of the Coming One whom John the Baptist proclaimed. We are told that many went from

"Jerusalem, and all Judea, and all the region round about Jordan, and were baptized of him in Jordan, confessing their sins" (Matt. 3: 5-6).

From the beginning baptism was intended in itself to be a form of confession. It is the public declaration of an inner experience, an active confession which all may witness. It openly declares that the one baptized was once a sinner, that he has now turned from a life of sin, that the old life has been buried with Christ, and that the new life has been raised to walk with Christ.

Why should any saved person shrink from baptism? It is one of the most beautiful ceremonies that has been given to men. To the one baptized it affords an experience of profound meaning. Who can ever get away from that hour when, standing before a crowd of people, he was lowered into a watery grave and raised to walk in newness of life? Again and again when Christian experience tends to grow cold the one who has undergone this experience of Christian baptism can recall it and renew love and devotion to the Christ who died, and was buried, and arose again for our sake. The confession of baptism points two ways—toward the sinner, who has been saved from sin, and toward the Saviour, who has given the new life. To miss this opportunity of confessing one's need of Christ and one's debt to him is to miss one of life's greatest privileges and opportunities.

3. Jesus Plainly Commands Public Confession

Jesus had very little patience with those who wanted to be his secret disciples. He said in language so plain that it cannot be misunderstood: "Whosoever therefore shall confess me before men, him will I confess also before my Father which is in heaven. But whosoever shall deny me before men, him will I also deny before my Father which is in heaven" (Matt. 10: 32).

Why should anyone want to be a secret disciple of Jesus Christ? Is it because he is ashamed of the Saviour? Listen to these words: "Whosoever therefore shall be ashamed of me and my words in this adulterous and sinful generation; of him also shall the Son of man be ashamed, when he cometh in the glory of his Father with the holy angels" (Mark 8: 38). Surely no one can be expected to be considered a real Christian who is ashamed of Christ.

Is it because he lacks courage? Here are plain words: "But the fearful, . . . shall have their part in the lake which burneth with fire and brimstone: which is the second death" (Rev. 21:8). In this verse the moral coward is placed in the same class with the "unbelieving, and the abominable, and murders, and whoremongers, and sorcerers, and idolaters, and all liars." How much faith has one who is too great a moral coward, to confess his faith?

Is refusal to confess Christ openly due to a sense of self-righteousness? Listen to these searching words: "For I say unto you, That except your righteousness shall exceed the righteousness of the scribes and Pharisees, ye shall in no case enter into the kingdom of heaven" (Matt. 5: 20). The Pharisees prided themselves on their morality. Their righteousness was self-righteousness. So good did they consider themselves that they felt no need of Jesus Christ and so rejected him. How can anyone expect to be saved if he thinks that he is in himself good enough to deserve salvation without Christ?

4. Confession, an Evidence of Salvation

Is confession a condition of salvation? Is there a certain amount of merit which comes through baptism which at least aids in salvation if it does not secure it? The answer is an emphatic "No!" If salvation depended to any degree whatsoever on confession and baptism then to that extent it would be of works and not of grace. We cannot purchase salvation by any amount of confession. We are not saved because we confess; we confess because we are saved.

Paul links confession and salvation in these words: "That if thou shalt confess with thy mouth the Lord Jesus, and shalt believe in thine heart that God hath raised him from the dead, thou shalt be saved" (Rom. 10: 9). The essential matter is clearly *heart belief*. But if there is genuine belief with the heart there will naturally follow confession with the mouth. This is true in every great experience as well as in the greatest of all experiences—salvation. If one is ill unto death and finds a doctor who cures him, nothing could keep him from telling others of the doctor who brought him from sickness and suffering back to health and life. It is a law of human life that when we have experienced some great blessing we immediately want to tell others about it.

Confession, to be convincing evidence of genuine salvation, must go farther than words. There is a great deal more in real confession than simply telling God, or someone else, that we have done wrong. Real confession goes deeper even than standing before a church congregation and admitting that one is a sinner and that he wants Christ to save him. Confession implies a changed life.

Suppose a boy who has been living in disobedience and sin should go to his father and say, "Father, I have a confession to make. I have been living a wicked life, and have been trying to deceive you. Won't you forgive me?" Then suppose that this boy, after having received his father's forgiveness and blessing, should go back the next night to the taverns and brothels that he had been accustomed to visit, and take up with the same old companions and live the same old life of dissipation and sin. What would you say about his confession? You would be bound to admit that it was a sham.

An honest confession of Christ means an honest turning away from sin and turning to a life of righteousness. He who is dead to sin is alive to righteousness; and he who is alive to righteousness is dead to sin. Paul makes this especially clear in the first five verses of the sixth chapter of Romans. Ought we not every now and then to search our hearts carefully to see if we are giving evidence of salvation through our daily confession of Christ?

III. COMMITTAL TO THE CHRISTIAN IDEAL

1. *The Ideal of Repentance*

The Bible is full of God's plain demand for repentance. Look up the following and similar passages: 2 Chronicles 7: 14; Psalm 24: 14, 18; Isaiah 65: 6-7; Matthew 4: 17; Luke 13: 5; Acts 3: 19. Jesus himself says, "Except ye repent, ye shall all likewise perish" (Luke 13: 3).

What is repentance? It comes from a word literally meaning "a change of mind." There is a story of a learned bishop who preached a deep theological sermon on repentance to a large but indifferent and sleepy audience. He came to the conclusion and was about to dismiss the congregation when a dear old retired preacher, sensing the fact that a great opportunity was being missed and, stirred by a sudden impulse, arose from his seat near the front and started down the aisle toward the door, crying at the top of his voice, "I'm going to hell! I'm going to hell!" The startled people thought the old man had suddenly gone crazy. When he reached the end of the aisle he started back and as he turned and walked toward the front of the church, with the light of heaven in his face, he cried again, "No, I've changed my mind. I'm going to heaven! I'm going to heaven! Oh, who will come and go with me, I'm bound for the promised land!" And then, with a few words of exhortation, he gave the invitation, and a number of people accepted Christ as their Saviour.

Repentance means the turning of one's life from unbelief and the love of sin to trust in Christ and surrender to him as Lord and Master. "Not the Christ living a life to be imitated, but the Christ giving a life to be appropriated lets us into the blessings of the gospel." The first step, according to Jesus himself, is a changed attitude toward sin. No one can be committed to a life of sin and to Christ at the same time.

2. *The Ideal of Faith*

Repentance and faith always go together in the Bible. They can no more be separated than the two sides of the same coin. Someone when asked which comes first, repentance or faith, replied that this would be like asking who enters the door first when John Smith comes in— John or Smith! In turning from sin, the sinner must have something to which to turn. Saving faith means the turning from sin and its power to Christ and his redemption.

It would be impossible even to begin to cite all the passages in the Bible which declare that faith is the fundamental of the Christian life. Just a few verses from the Gospel of John may be quoted: "For God so loved the world, that he gave his only begotten Son, that whosoever believeth in him should not perish, but have everlasting life. . . . He that believeth on him is not condemned: but he that believeth not is condemned already, because he hath not believed in the name of the only begotten Son of God. . . . He that believeth on the Son hath everlasting life: and he that believeth not the Son shall not see life; but the wrath of God abideth on him" (John 3: 16, 18, 36). (See also John 5: 24; 6: 47; 14: 12; 20: 30-31.)

What is saving faith? A father went down into a dark cellar. His little daughter called to him, saying, "Father, let me go with you!" The father replied, "All right, jump, and I will catch you." Without hesitation, although she could not see him, the child jumped and was safely caught in her father's arms. She might have believed that it was her father in the cellar, she might have believed that he could catch her if she jumped, but her faith proved itself when, at his word, she trusted where she could not see and obeyed where she could not know. Yet this was not blind faith, for she knew her father loved her and would not deceive her or let her come to harm.

Saving faith is like that; it is the committal of one-self, for time and eternity, to the saving power of Christ. The soul that does this must believe the gospel records concerning Christ, must accept him as the Son of God and the only Saviour, must trust him to do what he has promised, and then must act on this faith by openly becoming his follower. Such a faith is not blind, it is not contrary to reason, but is based on the claims of the Word of God and the character and atoning work of the Son of God. It is to this ideal of a life of faith that the Christian commits himself.

3. *The Ideal of Obedience*

The Christian life is a life of obedience. Throughout the Scriptures God demands implicit obedience on the part of those who call him Lord. Christ everywhere makes it clear that those who will not obey him cannot be his disciples.

What are the rewards of obedience? Does it pay to obey Christ? Do we get the most out of life when it is lived in accordance with this principle of loving obedience? Sometimes we may be tempted to doubt whether it is better to let Christ have his way or for us to have our own way. How shall we decide?

Jesus proposes that we compare the final outcome of two lives—the one of a man who hears his sayings and does them, the other of a man who hears Christ's words and does them not. The first man builds his house on a rock which withstands the storms that beat upon it. The second man builds his house upon the sand, and when the storm comes it falls and is destroyed. According to Jesus, obedience pays tremendously!

What is Christian obedience? A faithful old Negro, for many years a Christian, declared that while he did not know much, he knew enough to do what God told him. "But," someone argued, "suppose God were to tell you to jump through this stone wall. What would you do?" The old man replied simply: "I would jump.

Jumping would be my part, and getting through would be God's." But God does not call for impossible obedience. His commandments are always reasonable and just. The Christian life is not governed by a long and complicated set of rules. A half-dozen simple, fundamental principles will suffice for guidance: (1) Turn from sin and trust Christ as Saviour. (2) Confess Christ openly, in baptism and church membership. (3) Keep close to Christ through the study of his Word, through worship, through fellowship with his people. (4) Live a clean, upright life, in accordance with the Sermon on the Mount and the Golden Rule. (5) Be a good and faithful steward of time, talents, influence, possessions. (6) Win others to love and serve the Saviour.

When we became Christians we committed ourselves to this ideal of obedience. How true have we been to it? Let us hear Jesus challenge us again with the question, "Why call ye me, Lord, Lord, and do not the things which I say?" (Luke 6: 46).

4. *The Ideal of Unselfishness*

There are two conflicting claimants seeking to rule over every life. One of these is self and the other is Christ. If self rules Christ cannot; if Christ rules self cannot. The New Testament makes this clear in many great passages:

"Then said Jesus unto his disciples, If any man will come after me, let him deny himself, and take up his cross, and follow me" (Matt. 16: 24). "And thou shalt love the Lord thy God with all thy heart, and with all thy soul, and with all thy mind, and with all thy strength: this is the first commandment. And the second is like, namely this, Thou shalt love thy neighbor as thyself. There is none other commandment greater than these" (Mark 12: 30, 31). "This is my commandment, That ye love one another, as I have loved you. Greater love hath no man than this, that a man lay down his life for his friends" (John 15: 12-13).

What does it mean to live a life of unselfishness? In a certain home there were two daughters. One of them said to her mother, "Mother, I love you. Will you give me fifty cents to go to the picture show this evening?" The other said, "Mother, I love you. Now you sit down and rest while I wash the dishes." Both said, "I love you," but we know which one to believe. Christ has taught us to deny the claim of self, and to love others as he has loved us. John proposes this test: "We know that we have passed from death unto life, because we love the brethren. He that loveth not his brother abideth in death" (1 John 3: 14). Then he goes on to apply the test: "But whoso hath this world's good, and seeth his brother have need, and shutteth up his bowels of compassion from him, how dwelleth the love of God in him?" (1 John 3: 17.) And then he reaches this conclusion: "My little children, let us not love in word, neither in tongue; but in deed and in truth. . . . And this is his commandment, That we should believe on the name of his Son Jesus Christ, and love one another, as he gave us commandment" (1 John 3: 18, 23).

As Christians we have committed ourselves to this ideal of unselfish love for one another. Undoubtedly this is one of the most difficult Christian ideals to attain. Perhaps none of us lives up to it perfectly, but certainly it is an ideal which we ought constantly to hold before our eyes. There is not much prospect of winning others to Christ if selfishness rules our hearts and if the love of others is not our dominant motive. Can we honestly say that we are striving to attain this Christlike ideal?

5. *The Ideal of Service*

God had only one Son, and he sent him from heaven to earth to be a servant. Jesus declared, "I am among you as he that serveth" (Luke 22: 27). He took the lowly word "servant" and glorified it. He said, "The Son of man came not to be ministered unto but to minister" (Matt. 20: 28). He made service to others the test both of discipleship and of greatness in his kingdom. This ideal of service we find set forth in such passages as the following: "The disciple is not above his master, nor the servant above his lord" (Matt. 10: 24). "But Jesus called them unto him, and said, Ye know that the princes of the Gentiles exercise dominion over them, and they that are great exercise authority upon them. But it shall not be so among you: but whosoever will be great among you, let him be your minister; and whosoever will be chief among you, let him be your servant" (Matt. 20: 25, 27). "His lord said unto him, Well done, good and faithful servant; thou hast been faithful over a few things, I will make thee ruler over many things: enter thou into the joy of thy lord" (Matt. 25: 23).

The Christian is saved to serve. In the unselfish service of others he is most like his Master, and through this unselfish service the door is open for Christ to come into many hearts. The Christian who is always on the lookout for opportunities to help those in need, to minister to those who are sick, to comfort those who are in sorrow, and to do kindness to those whom he meets every day, will never be without opportunity to witness for Christ. Is it not strange that so many of us should have forgotten this ideal to which we committed ourselves when we accepted Christ? We need not expect our witness to be with power unless it is backed up by lives of unselfish service.

QUESTIONS FOR REVIEW AND CLASS DISCUSSION

1. Suppose someone should ask, "Just what do you mean by 'salvation'"? Give your answer in a few words.

2. What is "grace"? Why is it impossible for anyone to deserve salvation or to be saved because of good works and character?

3. Why is faith necessary to salvation? Are we saved by something we believe or by Christ in whom we believe?

4. If no good works, no changed character, no improved conduct appear after one professes conversion, what shall we conclude? What, then, is the relation of right living to salvation?

5. What would you say to those who claim to be Christians but have never publicly confessed Christ in baptism and church membership? What is the value of baptism?

6. Why does Jesus demand public confession? If a person does not hate sin enough to confess it nor love Christ enough to acknowledge him, what would be the natural conclusion? To whom should confession be made?

7. What is repentance? What are the evidences of true repentance? Why is repentance necessary to salvation?

8. What is saving faith? Why can there be no salvation without trusting Christ and believing his promises?

9. What is Christian obedience? Give a half-dozen ways in which the Christian should obey Christ. What are the rewards of obedience?

10. Why should the Christian live a life of unselfish service? What is the best proof that one has passed from death to life?

A COMPLETE WITNESS

OUTLINE

I. WITNESSING THROUGH CHRISTIAN HOME LIFE
1. Making the Home Truly Christian
2. Winning the Children to Christ
3. The Saving Influence of a Christian Home

II. WITNESSING THROUGH CHRISTIAN CITIZENSHIP
1. The Christian Citizen's Public Obligation
2. The Christian Citizen's Responsibility for the Welfare of Others
3. Wanted: Courageous Christian Citizens

III. WITNESSING THROUGH SACRIFICIAL GIVING
1. The Christian Measure of Giving
2. Strict Honesty in All Things

IV. THE STEWARDSHIP OF FAITHFUL TESTIMONY
1. The Terrible Guilt of Neglect
2. A Plea for Faithfulness to Souls
3. The Holy Spirit Longs to Bless Our Testimony

CHAPTER IV

A COMPLETE WITNESS

The world into which Jesus came was utterly selfish. Men lived for themselves with no thought of the welfare of others. The greatest man was the one who had the most servants, and success consisted in achieving power and authority. This fountain of selfishness had poured its streams of sin throughout the whole of human life. It was therefore literally a lost world into which Jesus came—a world which had missed the way of happiness, contentment, usefulness, goodness, blessedness. Jesus came to seek and to save this lost humanity. To do this he must inaugurate an absolutely opposite principle of life. Instead of selfishness as the chief motive, he proposed service as the new way of life for those who have been saved by faith in him. We turn now to a study of this new life of service to which Jesus calls those who follow him.

I. WITNESSING THROUGH CHRISTIAN HOME LIFE

The home is God's first and greatest institution. God established the home before he did the church, the state, the school, or any other of the institutions for the welfare and blessing of his human family.

As great as is this emphasis placed on the family in the Christian religion, the sad fact is that many Christians do not have happy, Christian homes. Never were there more perils which threaten our home life than today, and never was a true, strong, spiritual home life needed more than now. What are some of these dangers that threaten our home? The list is a long and discouraging one, including divorce, childless families, irreverent children, the breakdown of parental authority, the crowding together of people in tenements and apartments, constant moving from house to house and from community to community, extravagant spending, making the home just a place to eat and sleep, wrong purposes and motives, selfishness on the part of parents and children, lack of prayer and Bible reading, the disappearance of home religion.

1. *Making the Home Truly Christian*

It is not enough for father and mother and children to go to Sunday school and church together. If we would make our homes truly Christian we must realize that Christianity is a life, not just a matter of nominal church membership and attendance on public services of religion. Indeed, a family may attend church and then come home to complain and criticize so that all the good that might have been accomplished through the preaching and teaching is nullified by the bad attitudes that find expression in criticism and gossip.

The importance of the home from the standpoint of the fruits that it produces in personal character and in the social order is forcefully brought out in this searching paragraph: "A family is humanity's great opportunity to walk the way of the cross. Mothers know that; some fathers know it; some children grow up to learn it. In homes where this is true, where all other aims are subordinated to this one of making the home count for high character, to training lives into right social adjustment and service, the primary emphasis is not on times and seasons for religion; religion is the life of that home, and in all its common living every child learns the way of the great Life of all. The good man comes out of the good home—the home that is good in character, aim, and organization, not occasionally but permanently—the home where the religious spirit, the spirit of idealism, and the sense of the infinite and divine are diffused rather than injected. The inhuman, anti-social vampires, who suck their brothers' blood, whether they be called magnates or mob-leaders, grafters or gutter thieves, often learned to take life in terms of graft by the attitude and atmosphere of their homes."[1]

2. *Winning the Children to Christ*

One of the dangers that we as Christian parents face today is that of passing our spiritual responsibility for the children over to somebody else. When a baby is born we let his name be placed on the cradle roll. Soon the little fellow is old enough to begin the successive promotions through the various departments of the church's training program. During this time he is enrolled in the various church organizations—Sunday school, Training Union, and the Sunbeam Band. Perhaps he will join the Boy Scouts, and will spend several weeks each summer in Vacation Bible school.

Somehow we drift into the feeling that all will be well with the child if he attends with more or less regularity these various church meetings and takes part in these religious educational activities. Could anything be more dangerous than this? The greatest single responsibility entrusted of Almighty God to a father and a mother is that of leading their own child toward Christ, to Christ, and into the service of Christ.

Dr. Albert W. Beaven, in a most helpful little book, *Fireside Talks for the Family Circle*, takes us back to that sacred experience when the first baby was born into his home. "Then I began to realize that that little babe, lying so still in my arms and whose tiny hand clasped my finger so caressingly, had placed upon us a new and solemn demand. I knelt in prayer that night by the bedside of the mother, and we two prayed for the little life which God had given to us."

Does not this picture recall to many of us recollections of a similar experience? Have we somehow got away from the sacred impulses that came to us as we looked into the faces of our children when they first came? Doctor Beaven states for us the truth that appeals to

[1]Cope, H. F., *Religious Education in the Family*, Chicago, University of Chicago Press, p. 6. Now out of print.

our conscience as well as our intellect when, continuing, he says: "Religious training of childhood is a first duty for Christian parents. We cannot turn it over to anyone else. Certainly we cannot look to the school nor the state for the inculcating of great religious ideals and convictions. They are not permitted to teach religion. Nor can we shift the burden to the church—that marvelous institution which for two thousand years has been gathering children within its walls and instructing them in the things of God. The church that is on the corner can help us, but 'the church that is our house' is the institution to which we must first look, and as we are responsible for the functioning of that church we must accept the challenge."

3. The Saving Influence of a Christian Home

Paul, writing to Timothy, the young minister, bases his confidence in him on the fact that from a child he has known the Holy Scriptures, which are able to make wise unto salvation through faith in Christ Jesus (2 Timothy 3: 15). Someone once asked a learned doctor how early he thought the Christian training of a child should begin. He answered quickly, "With its grandmother!" The child must repent and believe for himself, but it would be impossible to overestimate the advantage of a child who has been reared in a Christian atmosphere and who has been led toward Christ from the first moment of his life. The noblest of our ministers and missionaries, almost without exception, came out of Christian homes.

Dr. William W. Faris, in his charming little book, *The Christian Home,* estimates that not more than one home out of ten is a home of piety, regular churchgoing, and family prayer. Yet, he points out, this one-tenth of our homes produces fully nine-tenths of the men and women whom the world delights to honor—of men whom the people push into leadership, and the women whom multitudes trust and revere. "Do you know of a single

*Now out of print.

family that has survived in honor of decency for three successive generations without at least one household in the line given to the ways of religion?" he asks. He declares that he has never been able to learn of a single instance. "But," he continues, "on the other hand, known to all careful observers, the bone and sinew of Christendom is predominantly made up of products of families in which habits of domestic and professed piety are carefully handed on from generation to generation. The vital and tremendous significance of this is obvious."

This truth is now perfectly clear: If we would be the sort of Christians that we want to be, exerting influence for Christ and winning others to him, we must have the backing of a Christian home life. Another truth, equally great, is this: If we would rear a generation of Christian workers to take our places, the men and women of the future who will carry on the work of the churches and extend the limits of the kingdom of God, we must produce them in the atmosphere and from the soil of Christian homes.

II. WITNESSING THROUGH CHRISTIAN CITIZENSHIP

These questions are often asked: Ought a Christian take part in politics? If so, what are his obligations as a Christian citizen? Politics, properly understood, is the science of government. Government can be either good or bad. If it is good, conditions are much more favorable for human welfare and the progress of Christ's kingdom. If conditions are bad, sin rears its ugly head and strikes at human happiness and the program of Christ's church. Can the Christian, if he is loyal to the interests of Christ and humanity, shirk his duty as a citizen? If all Christians should wash their hands of responsibility for good government and for the public welfare, it follows that authority would fall into the hands of evil men. Has not this actually happened in many cases where government has come under the control of dishonest and corrupt politicians whose influence has been for evil in the life of the nation, the state, and the community?

1. *The Christian Citizen's Public Obligation*

More than once Jesus faced his obligation as a citizen of the Roman Empire. An instance is given in Matthew 17: 24-27 (read this passage).

Jesus Christ, through whom the world was made, might have claimed exemption from the payment of taxes, but he insisted, as a good citizen, on paying the tribute money. He taught respect for and obedience to the constituted authorities, so long as their demands did not run contrary to conscience. The early Christians were law-abiding citizens, preferring to obey the law even when it was unjust rather than to rebel against established government.

Paul's letter to Titus turns to the practical matter of good citizenship. Titus must not forget to preach on this practical and pressing subject. Christians are citizens of two kingdoms—the kingdom of heaven, and the kingdom of this world. The preacher must not overlook this earthly citizenship, but as he brings the message of Christ to the Christian community he should "put them in mind to be subject to principalities and powers, to obey magistrates, to be ready to every good work."

What is the Christian citizen's public obligation? It is to respect officers of the law, and to be a law-abiding citizen. Even though civil authorities be unworthy and laws be unjust, the Christian citizen is not to rebel and fight, but patiently to bear wrong until, by peaceful methods of persuasion and influence, he can get bad conditions changed. Ought we not to give more attention than most of us now do to this question of our public obligation as Christian citizens?

2. *The Christian Citizen's Responsibility for the Welfare of Others*

The heart of the matter lies just here: the Christian citizen must put the welfare of others ahead of his private gain. Perhaps this is the hardest single lesson that he has set us to learn. When we become Christians we enrol in this school of unselfishness, but we have a hard time all our lives learning our lessons and passing our examinations. There is scarcely a day in which we are not tempted to think of ourselves first, to put our interests ahead of the interests of our neighbors, forgetting Christ's great law that whosoever would come after him must deny himself, and take up his cross, and follow him.

At the very foundation of a true democracy is this principle of sacrifice for the common good. Democratic government, Abraham Lincoln wisely said, is of the people, by the people, and for the people. No man nor group of men can prosper at the expense of another man or another group and be a good citizen. The ideal which upheld our forefathers in those dark days when they were fighting for our national independence was that of "liberty, equality, fraternity." All men, they declared, are created free and equal, and no government can endure which does not recognize this self-evident truth.

Jesus set forth this principle with strong emphasis. On one occasion, when the apostles were disputing over rank, he called them to him, and pointed out that they were not to be as the Gentiles, who lord it over one another. "But whosoever will be great among you, let him be your minister" (Matt. 20: 26). What, then, is to be the proof of the new life in Christ? In words as strong as language can declare it, Paul affirms that "they which have believed in God might be careful to maintain good works" (Titus 3: 8). In other words, the good citizen is the man or the woman whose life produces fruits that are "good and profitable unto men."

3. *Wanted: Courageous Christian Citizens*

There has developed an attitude among a good many people today which expresses itself like this: "Don't do anything. Don't say anything. Don't take sides. It might get you into trouble." Is this the attitude of the Christian citizen? Can we be really Christian if we refuse to stand for the right because to do so might involve us in difficulty? We shrink from entangling ourselves in the troubles of others, and especially do we dislike to have our quiet routine disturbed by having to take sides in an issue. But if this issue is right against wrong, the powerful against the weak, the devil against God, the world against Christ and his church, then what sort of soldiers of the King will we be if we pass by on the other side for the sake of our own comfort and safety? Jesus said plainly, "He that is not with me is against me." As a matter of fact, when a moral principle is at stake, to be neutral is in reality to get on the other side.

Never did graver questions face thoughtful Christian citizens than those which confront us now. It is not always easy to know what is right and best. An editorial writer in a recent daily newspaper makes this thoughtful comment which we as Christians and church members may well take to heart: "Life about us calls to us constantly for help from its man-made injustice and cruelty, which can only be destroyed as men of goodwill have the courage to fight for and with their brothers. In such situations, a man who refuses to risk anything of his own will find that, slowly but surely, his own spirit is shriveling and he is becoming something less than a man."

III. Witnessing Through Sacrificial Giving

Ours is a property-centered age. The great majority of people today spend the greater part of their waking time dealing with property or its money equivalent. Life can scarcely be lived without constant reference to the *things* which men possess. Stewardship has been defined as our use of property for God's ends. "Property and possessions may be difficult to define, but we clearly mean by them the things we are free to control. Stewardship views this control in the light of three great facts: (1) Property is God's and so it must honor him. (2) Property is social and intended for the advance of society. (3) Property is personal and must help personality to come into its own."

1. *The Christian Measure of Giving*

How much shall I give? Often this question really means, How little can I get by with? Many church members have learned that they can "get by" with giving nothing at all. They congratulate themselves that they have saved that much, and have it to use for something else. There are others who feel that they must give something, but what they give is the leftover from all their other spending. To a multitude of church members all giving is more or less painful. It hurts them when the preacher mentions money in the sermon, and they complain when approached for their subscription to the budget that the church is always after money! Some give as an excuse for staying away from church that all the church wants is their money, and since they have none to give they will just stay at home. For all these the joy of living is lost, and even greater is the loss of usefulness, of growth in grace, and of God's approval upon their lives.

How much shall I give? To an inner circle of faithful Christians this question means, How little can I get along on for myself? They realize that they must give sensibly, taking into account their obligations and the necessities of life. Their chief concern is to spend as little as possible on themselves in order that they may have all the more to give to Christ. They are unwilling to waste money, or to spend it extravagantly, because they recognize that it all belongs to God and they dare not throw his money away for that which is unnecessary. The more they give the happier they are, and they are constantly on the lookout for investments for their Heavenly Father that will bring good returns for the kingdom of his Son. Such Christians have found the joy of giving, and are building character that will withstand all the storms of life.

2. *Strict Honesty in All Things*

Christian stewardship is based on strict honesty. There must be honesty in acquiring wealth, honesty in investing it, honesty in using it, honesty in giving it, and honesty in accounting for it after it has been given. It is not enough that money be generously given. Christian stewardship demands that it be acquired in accordance with the principles of Christ and that it be used in line with New Testament standards. Has there not been too much separation in our day between the getting and using of money, and the ideals of Christianity?

Paul was exceedingly careful in his handling of the money which was entrusted to him to be taken for the relief of the Christians at Jerusalem. He insisted that someone be chosen by the churches to go along with him, in order to avoid any possible criticism of the way in which he administered the relief fund. He made the same demand upon himself that he made upon others, that every precaution should be taken for "providing for honest things, not only in the sight of the Lord, but also in the sight of men." It would increase the confidence of those who give if all those who handle their gifts should fix this standard of Paul's, to the end that no question should ever arise concerning the distribution of the money which came into their hands. Church treasurers, and secretaries, and finance committees, and denominational boards are stewards of the money entrusted to them by the churches, and should administer every dollar in such a way as to be wholly above suspicion. What a great thing it would be for every church member and every church if these stewardship principles of Paul were earnestly preached and persistently practiced!

IV. The Stewardship of Faithful Testimony

The plan of Jesus for the spread of Christianity is amazingly simple: *Each one a winning witness.* Jesus won John and Andrew. John won James, and Andrew won Peter. Together they won Philip and Nathanael. Thus the number of disciples grew until there were twelve, then seventy, then one hundred and twenty, then at Pentecost three thousand were added, this number being soon increased to five thousand, after which the count is lost as the number grows to "a multitude."

If each Christian in the world today should go forth determined to win others, and each should succeed, how long would it be before the whole world was won to Christ? This generation would not pass away before Christ's Great Commission would be carried out!

1. *The Terrible Guilt of Neglect*

In ancient times every city had its watchtower. It was the business of the watchman to keep constantly on the lookout to discover the approach of an invading army or a marauding band of robbers. If the watchman grew careless, or fell asleep, and the city was taken by surprise, the guilty watchman was accounted worthy of death.

Ezekiel, the prophet, lived and prophesied during the exile of Israel about the sixth century, B.C. God called him to minister to his Jewish people who were in Babylonian captivity. Would all to whom Ezekiel brought God's message repent and be saved? No; many would reject the message, while only a few would receive it. What, then, would be the prophet's responsibility? It would be that of the watchman, to give the warning message. But suppose the prophet should fail to give the warning, neglecting or refusing to warn the wicked from his wicked way, then what? "The same wicked man shall die in his iniquity; but his blood will I require at thine hand."

Let us recall the experience of conversion. Who prayed for us? Who came and spoke to us? Who warned us of the consequences of sin, and begged us to accept the Saviour? Suppose no one had been interested in us, no one had prayed for us or spoken to us; do you suppose we would be Christians today? Then what if we never pray for the lost, never seek out and speak to one who is without Christ; is it not altogether possible that some will go into a Christless eternity who might have made their home forever with God had we been faithful? Let these questions sink into our hearts as we meditate upon the terrible guilt of neglect.

2. *A Plea for Faithfulness to Souls*

A brilliant English essayist said recently that if he believed what Christians claim to believe about eternal life and eternal death, he would crawl across England if necessary, on his hands and knees, to get his friends and loved ones to accept Christ. How many Christians truly believe that those without Christ are eternally lost? If any one of us should see a man, even though a perfect stranger, about to walk in front of a fast approaching automobile that would dash him to his death, would we not cry out to him, and even rush to his side to stop him? Yet we live daily with those who are on the brink of eternal death and never so much as raise our voices to warn them of their danger or to tell them the way of eternal life.

Paul believed what he preached. He did not stop with the delivering of two sermons on the sabbath and the conducting of a midweek prayer meeting. He did not wait for people to come to hear his message, but went from house to house, dealing personally with both Jews and Greeks, beseeching them with many tears to repent and believe. One can picture this grand old soul-winner, having poured out his soul in reasoning to no effect, bursting into tears in his deep concern for the lost soul with whom he was dealing. And where logic and persuasion failed, the tears of Paul no doubt often won. How long has it been since we wept over lost souls whom we longed to win to Christ?

3. *The Holy Spirit Longs to Bless Our Testimony*

Into a telephone exchange run wires from many directions. One lifts the receiver, desiring to talk to someone at a distance. But nothing happens until the operator makes the connection at the central office. The Holy Spirit may be compared to the operator in the telephone exchange. It is he who rings the bell, so to speak, in the Christian's heart calling him to speak to someone who wants him at the other end of the line. In the case of Peter and Cornelius the Holy Spirit heard the call of the Roman soldier for someone to bring him the saving message; and then he had to get the attention of Peter in order that the gospel might be made known to this seeking soul. When Peter arrived at the home of Cornelius he found that the way had been prepared for his message by the Holy Spirit, and that the Holy Spirit was there in mighty power to bless his testimony for Christ.

Perhaps the chief reason why we Christians hesitate to speak to others about Christ is that we somehow think we must do it in our own strength. We forget that the Holy Spirit is at work in the hearts of the lost, making them dissatisfied, causing them to want peace and forgiveness, and opening their hearts to the gospel message. When the impulse comes to speak to a lost person about his soul, we may be sure that this impulse is from the Holy Spirit, and if obeyed will be received by a heart that the Holy Spirit has been preparing for our witness. Ought we not, then, to press the case with holy boldness, knowing that we have One who stands alongside to help us?

QUESTIONS FOR REVIEW AND CLASS DISCUSSION

1. Jesus taught us to pray, "Thy kingdom come. Thy will be done in earth, as it is in heaven" (Matt. 6:10). Name some of the aspects of life, other than individual, which would have to be changed if this prayer were realized?

2. What are some of the dangers that threaten home life today? What are some of the consequences when the home fails?

3. Who are more responsible than all others for the winning of children to Christ? What mistaken notions of their duty to their children do many Christian parents have?

4. How may the Christian family be restored to its place of primal importance in evangelism and Christian nurture? Give several specific suggestions.

5. Why should Christians take an active part in politics? State a half-dozen public obligations of the Christian citizen.

6. State some of the respects in which Christians are responsible for the welfare of others. What is the weakness of evangelism that seeks to get people saved but is not concerned for the kind of lives they live afterward?

7. How would you state the doctrine of stewardship? Why should a person have the duty of giving made plain while he is being won to Christ?

8. Why ought Christians to be strictly honest? When is the best time to get a person started on a life policy of thorough honesty toward God and man?

9. To what does "stewardship" refer besides money? How are we to discharge our stewardship of faithful testimony?

10. What is our guilt if souls perish whom we should have brought to Christ? How does the Holy Spirit help us to be good witnesses?

MOTIVE AND METHOD

OUTLINE

I. MOTIVE THAT IMPELS TO MASTERY

   1. Love, the Master Motive
   2. The Art of Soul-Winning Can Be Learned

II. APPLYING BUSINESS PRINCIPALS TO EVANGELISM

   1. What Are the Chief Requisites of a Good Salesman?
   2. How Should He Approach a Prospective Customer?
   3. What Should Inspire Him to Sell His Goods?

III. METHODS OF APPROACH TO THE LOST

   1. Planning the Best Approach
   2. Making a Favorable Contact
   3. Breaking Down Barriers
   4. The Necessity for Patience and Perseverance

IV. BRINGING TO DECISION AND ACTION

   1. Delay, the Devil's Last Stronghold
   2. The Futility of Over-persuasion
   3. Strengthening Courage and Determination
   4. Leading to Baptism and Church Membership

MOTIVE AND METHOD

Scarcely anything is more important than the Christian worker's motives. A motive is that which moves. What the motor is to the automobile or the locomotive is to the train the Christian's motive is to his work as a soul-winner. Winning another to Christ is a deeply personal matter, and cannot be done in a perfunctory and professional manner. It is therefore of the utmost importance, as we undertake this supreme task of personal soul-winning, that our motives be true and right. Let us frankly and honestly examine our motives as Christian workers, seeking to make them acceptable to God, approved of Christ, and in line with the purposes of the Holy Spirit.

I. MOTIVE THAT IMPELS TO MASTERY

1. *Love, the Master Motive*

There are a great many motives that control our lives. There is the motive of self-importance. Every normal human being wants to feel that he is important, that he amounts to something, that people pay attention to him. Then there is the motive of self-gratification. We all like to please ourselves, to have our own way, to get what we want. Again, there is the motive of self-interest. It is human nature to want to do that for which we will get the largest return for ourselves. Even church work may have in it a certain amount of appeal to self-interest. It is easy to fall into the attitude of expecting to get something in return for everything we do, even our Christian service.

Are these motives sufficient? Will they sustain us day in and day out? Experience and observation prove conclusively that unless there is a higher motive than any of these we lose interest, grow discouraged, and quit. One of the sad things about church work is that there are so many "quitters." Every now and then we find someone who was once an active, enthusiastic Christian worker who has grown inactive and cold. How account for this change? In nearly every instance it gets back to the fact of inadequate motive. If the motive had self as its center and Christ in the circumference, there came inevitable conflict between the self-motive and the Christ-motive. If the self-motive won out, the Christian worker lost out. If the Christ-motive became victorious, the Christian worker won the victory.

What, then, is the Christian worker's master-motive? Let us turn to these Scripture passages for the answer:

"He that hath my commandments, and keepeth them, he it is that loveth me: and he that loveth me shall be loved of my Father, and I will love him, and will manifest myself to him . . . Jesus answered and said unto him, If a man love me, he will keep my words: and my Father will love him, and we will come unto him, and make our abode with him" (John 14: 21, 23).

"For to me to live is Christ, and to die is gain" (Phil. 1: 21).

"For the love of Christ constraineth us; because we thus judge, that if one died for all, then were all dead" (2 Cor. 5: 14).

Shall we not dare to believe it? Shall we not with holy boldness link our poor human love with God's infinite love in Christ to bring souls to spiritual birth? This is God's amazing offer of partnership. Let us humbly and gladly accept it!

2. The Art of Soul-Winning Can Be Learned

One of the devil's best tricks is to delude Christians into the belief that they are not fitted to be soul-winners, and that this delicate and difficult business must be left to a small group of "experts." True, soul-winning is an art, but it is an art which any Christian can learn. What is necessary in order to learn how to be a successful personal worker?

(1) A genuine experience of grace. One must be truly saved himself before he can lead another to the Saviour.

(2) Love of Christ and of souls. One cannot lead another to love one whom he does not love, nor can he win people unless he loves people.

(3) Willingness to be used of the Holy Spirit. One dare not deal with a matter of such importance in his own strength and wisdom, but must yield himself to the Holy Spirit's guidance.

(4) Making and utilizing every possible occasion. One must not trust to chance, but must plan to make contacts with those whom he would reach. Then he must make use of every apparently chance-occasion for opening up the subject that will lead to a faithful witness for Christ.

(5) Knowledge of the way of salvation. One must know the simple doctrines of grace which make clear how Christ saves the sinner.

(6) Continual practice based on sound theory. One must learn by much experience, and study constantly the experiences of others as given in the best available books.

(7) Definite, unceasing intercessory prayer. One must have a list of people for whom he is especially concerned, and take these individuals to God in prayer that his weakness may be reinforced by divine strength.

The majority of men and women who make up our churches are daily associated with modern business, either as buyers or as sellers, or both. Their training, by daily experience, is in the field of business practice. A Christian Church is more than a business enterprise, it is a business institution, and is in the greatest business in the world. A church owns property, it raises and spends money, it seeks to enlist, organize, and utilize a great number of workers, and it undertakes to get people to accept its goods—the gospel of Jesus Christ and all its fruits. There are business principles which have been developed through centuries of trade that can be applied with wisdom and profit to the supreme business of the church, the winning of souls.

II. Applying Business Principles to Evangelism

A few years ago Rev. Christian J. Reisner, a well-known soul-winning pastor, conceived the idea of addressing a set of questions to a group of outstanding present-day Christian businessmen. He picked out the replies of nine businessmen high in both business and church circles, the men chosen being J. C. Penney, of the Penney Chain Stores; Will H. Hays, former postmaster-general and chairman of the motion picture industry; Percy S. Straus, vice-president of R. H. Macy & Company; Arthur Capper, United States Senator and wealthy publisher; J. L. Kraft, of the Kraft-Phenix Cheese Company; Joseph P. Day, internationally known real-estate salesman; Stanley Resor, president of one of the largest advertising agencies in the world; Frederick H. Ecker, president of the Metropolitan Life Insurance Company; E. C. Sams, president of the J. C. Penney Company. Let us look at some of the questions which they were asked, their answers, and the comments made by Pastor Reisner on their replies:

1. *What Are the Chief Requisites of a Good Salesman?*

Penney—(1) Character. (2) Personality.

Capper—(1) Intelligence, honesty, and energy. (2) Pleasing personality, with ability to meet various kinds of persons and impress them favorably.

Kraft—(1) Knowledge of the merchandise to be sold. (2) Ability to close a sale.

Resor—(1) Ability to think clearly in terms of the relation to his prospect of what the salesman has to sell. (2) Ability to talk clearly and interestingly.

2. How Should He Approach a Prospective Customer?

Penney—In a pleasing manner that will inspire confidence in the salesman and in the house he represents, and above all, make the customer feel at home.

Straus—With confidence in his knowledge and ability, and with an attitude that will create a pleasant impression on the customer.

Kraft—By introducing himself and his line; then going straight to the point and presenting his proposition.

Sams—With an open countenance that will immediately command respect—one that will inspire confidence.

3. What Should Inspire Him to Sell His Goods?

Hays—He is prompted by the knowledge that he has something which will add happiness to the life of the man who buys his goods.

Resor—A firm belief in the merchandise or service he is selling; that is, a belief not only in its intrinsic value, but its value to the person to whom he is selling it. With such a knowledge he can know that he is not only doing a necessary part of the world's work, but is contributing to its progress.[1]

Every requisite of the good salesman as given by these business executives finds its counterpart in the equipment of the successful soul-winner. Shall we, who are in the greatest business in the world, be satisfied with less skill and ability than men of affairs display in "selling" that which perishes with the using? Study these statements, and then determine how each one may be applied to personal evangelism.

---

[1]Reisner, Christian, *Disciple Winners*, Chapter I.

III. Methods of Approach to the Lost

1. *Planning the Best Approach*

The skilful physician seeking co-operation from his patient, carefully plans his approach. The capable lawyer, undertaking to secure the desired decision, carefully plans his approach to judge and jury. The successful salesman, bent on selling his goods to the prospective customer, gives much time and thought to an effective approach. Ought the children of the world to be permitted to prove themselves wiser than we the children of light?

The personal worker, before undertaking the tremendously serious business of winning a soul to Christ, should raise with himself certain questions like unto these: Am I impressed that the Holy Spirit wants me to speak to this individual? Have I prayed for guidance? What do I know about this man or woman? What interests do we have in common? Is this person interested in spiritual things, or is he indifferent or antagonistic? How may I win his confidence? What Scripture passages would probably be most effective? What mutual acquaintance could I get who would reinforce me? What difficulties seem to stand in the way of this person's becoming a Christian? How could these difficulties best be overcome?

Thoughtfully and prayerfully the Christian worker should ponder such questions as these, perhaps writing out the answers in brief notes in his "Personal Worker's Notebook." Think of the advantage of such thoughtful preparation in advance as over against haphazard conversation with people whom we just casually meet!

2. *Making a Favorable Contact*

It is a truism that, as a rule, we must win the lost to ourselves before we can win them to our Saviour. If the unsaved person in whom I am interested does not believe in me, does not like me, or holds himself aloof from me, it is next to impossible to influence him to accept Christ. Someone else may do it, but I cannot. It is therefore of utmost importance that we seek to be winsome, friendly, attractive in manner and in personality. What makes one person attractive to another? Not necessarily physical or intellectual or social charm. The one certain way to be attractive to another is to take a deep, genuine interest in the welfare of that person. If I can convince anybody that I am interested in him, that I like him for his own sake, that I believe he has possibilities; if I can get him to talk about himself, to reveal his aspirations and ambitions, to confide his hopes and fears; then he will assume toward me a friendly attitude.

A pastor-evangelist of wide experience says that in planning to reach a given individual we should consider the who? how? what? and where? of it all. "First, who can reach the man best? Some men are approachable with one who are not with another. How are we to approach men? Some by appointment, others by happenstance, some boldly, directly, frankly; others in general statements and quietly. Here more than anywhere else common-sense intuition must be exercised. But, what are we to say to them? What are we to do? Just as necessary as these questions are their opposites. What are we to refrain from saying? What are we to refrain from doing? The best way to convince some men of the reality of the Christian faith is to keep still and let them talk. It is not always what we say. Truth does not need a defender, nor theology an apologist. A great many times a quiet, gentle spirit wins when a brainy argument drives away. When shall we make the approach? Wise men always plan their time. You must sometimes wait for the right time for years. Watch for that time— God's time! Where? Seek to get men to the places where they are naturally impressed; among the companions who will help. It may be a walk together, or a vacation together, or an evening call, or a quiet Sunday afternoon. If possible get your man alone, and talk to him where there can be no possible interruption.

Never hurry; take plenty of time. If not successful once, come back and back again."[2]

3. Breaking Down Barriers

There is something that stands between every sinner and the Saviour. It is not enough to say that this is *sin*. Sin takes many forms and must be dealt with in many ways. Just what is the wall of partition that separates between the soul of an unsaved friend and the Saviour who is ready and willing to save him? It is of very great importance to get this obstacle clearly out in the open, examine it, and then find the way, if possible, to remove it.

Often the unsaved person does not know exactly what the difficulty is. Perhaps there is so much wrong in his life that he cannot single out any particular thing. Perhaps, on the other hand, he does not feel conscious of sin in his life, and must have it revealed to him. Perhaps the difficulty is practical; or it may be intellectual; or it may be emotional; or it may be indefinable. Get your unsaved friend to talk freely about himself—his parents, his early home life, his youthful struggles, his ambitions and disappointments, his satisfactions and dissatisfactions. As he talks, try to get him to see the hand of God in his life, and what he has missed by not having a Saviour to rely on, the Holy Spirit's guidance, and the Bible's unerring wisdom. Be sure not to criticize, nor to argue. Quietly ask if he is satisfied with himself, if he thinks God will be satisfied with the account he gives of himself at the judgment, if he has treated Christ fairly and given his own soul a decent chance? Lead him to see that there is no barrier too great for Christ to break down, nor is there any difficulty too great for Christ to meet. Then, if possible, lead to the positive desire for divine help, which opens the way for simple and sincere prayer. Press for immediate decision if the time seems to be ripe, but always leave the door open for further conversation and appeal.

---

[2]Stone, John Timothy, *Recruiting for Christ*, pp. 102, 103.

4. *The Necessity for Patience and Perseverance*

A veteran soul-winner advises against making the error of persisting in winning men the first time you call. "Almost invariably," he says, "you will lose them. Win a man's confidence, no matter how long it takes. Then the matter of winning his soul and life will not be difficult. The greatest surgeons are the men who are never hurried in their private offices. Scores may be waiting without, but their best attention is given to the individual case; and in winning victory over disease, repeated treatment and operation may be necessary. This is also true in reaching men in business. I had an insurance man call upon me thirteen times before he wrote a policy, and then I did not want the policy half so much as I wanted to remain in his good graces, for he had become a friend. It would hardly be fair to say I wanted to get rid of him. Win the confidence of men. Show your sincerity, your persistency, your determination, but show it wisely, sympathetically. Don't try to wholesale your work— retail it. Take time for prayer and thought. In entering a 'tournament of activity' don't try to win the whole series in one game. Omit your argument—show heart rather than head. Use earnestness, and don't be afraid of genuine feeling and emotion."

Are we not prone to give up too easily? A successful insurance agent says that he sometimes makes as many as forty to fifty contacts before he at length sells his prospect a policy. Wise business and professional men cultivate "good-will" as they look many years ahead to future business. We are in this campaign for souls until Christ calls us home or comes again. There is no place for discouragement nor impatience, for we know that we shall reap if we faint not.

IV. Bringing to Decision and Action

1. *Delay, the Devil's Last Stronghold*

When Paul, on trial for his life and liberty before Agrippa, began to bore into the king's conscience, Festus, the governor, interrupted with the cry, "Paul, thou art beside thyself; much learning doth make thee mad." Then, as Paul pressed the case for Jesus Christ, King Agrippa said, "Almost thou persuadest me to be a Christian." Whereupon Paul said, "I would to God, that not only thou, but also all that hear me this day, were both almost, and altogether such as I am, except these bonds." (See Acts 26: 24-29.)

Like Felix, whom Paul sought in vain to win to a decision for Christ, are uncounted multitudes of souls that are forever lost because they waited for "a more convenient season." Delay is now and has ever been the devil's last stronghold. No matter what else might occur, how many sermons may be heard, or how many good resolutions made, he is satisfied if he can just get people to put off making a decision. Dr. Roland Q. Leavell, in his excellent book, *Winning Others to Christ,* relates how a revival was sweeping through the student body in the college where Aaron Burr was in attendance. Young Burr was almost persuaded to become a Christian. He consulted a professor, telling of his inclination toward committing his all to Jesus Christ. The professor thought he should appear thoughtful and scholarly, so he said, "Mr. Burr, you are in an abnormal state of mind, being affected by this great wave of emotion which is sweeping the campus. You are a man of intellect. Why not wait until this has passed away and then clearly think through your religious problem?" Aaron Burr said that was exactly what he would do. And never again did anyone ever hear of Aaron Burr being concerned for one single moment about his relationship to Jesus Christ. What a difference it would have made had pressure for decision brought Aaron Burr to Christ! And what a difference it would have made with thousands who are now in hell if they had broken through the barrier of indecision and taken their stand for Christ before it was too late!

2. *The Futility of Over-persuasion*

It is interesting to note that Jesus never begged anyone to accept him. We have no record in the New
Testament of any of the apostles, or of any other Christian witness, having pushed and pulled, or teased and
threatened in the effort to get someone to decide for
Christ. Jesus looked upon the rich young ruler and loved
him; he appealed to the young man's best self; but when
the young man turned sadly away, Jesus let him go.

Mr. Edward L. Pell, in his excellent book, *How Can I
Lead My Pupils to Christ?* points out that importunity
has accomplished many things, but it has never led a
soul to decide for Christ. It may lead a person to say
he will decide for Christ, but that, he points out, is a
different matter. Continuing, Mr. Pell points out that
he would, with all the urging of love, tell the person
with whom he is dealing that the time has come to decide for Christ, and would try to set before him a picture of Christ that would draw him. "But under no
circumstances," he declares, "would I say, 'Please, please
do; for Mother's sake, or my sake, please decide for
Christ today.' Our success in winning for Christ depends
not on our persistence as beggars, but rather upon our
ability to present Christ in a way that will pull upon
the heart strings." Let us not, in our zeal and enthusiasm,
substitute human persuasion for the regenerating power
of the Holy Spirit.

3. *Strengthening Courage and Determination*

It takes courage to break with sin and unbelief and
step out before the world to declare oneself a Christian.
There are men who would face mortal danger without a
quiver whose hearts fail them as they confront the or-
deal of making a public profession of religion and sub-
mitting to the rite of baptism. There are timid women
who have gone down into the valley of death without
fear who shrink with almost uncontrollable dread from

*Now out of print.

the thought of making themselves a spectacle in coming forward to confess Christ and to be received into the church. There are children and young people who become unaccountably frightened as they picture themselves taking publicly a step that commits them to Christ and his ideals when they are not sure that they can live up to their profession.

Then, too, the decision for Christ requires a high measure of determination. There is a new way of life to be entered into, there are new habits to be formed, there are new associations to be made, there are new duties to perform. For adults particularly the power of habit is very strong. Equally strong is the inertia, the habit of doing nothing, that must now be replaced with activity in the service of Christ and of others. The will that has not been exercised in Christian activities is weak. Even when one longs to be a Christian, there is lack of determination to turn away from the old life and enter into the new. The majority of people need help in the strengthening of their determination to become Christians.

It is at this point that human aid steps in. Courage is strengthened by companionship. It is a well-known fact that people will brave danger together that they would not meet if left alone. In the divine arithmetic, one shall chase a thousand, but two shall put ten thousand to flight. At the crucial moment of decision there is need for the warm handclasp of encouragement, the energizing of determination through approval and sympathy, and the breaking down of indecision through the contagion of example. To say, "I have done this, and you can do it, too," and then to reinforce wavering decision by sympathy and prayer is to provide that strength of courage and determination often necessary for the final step.

4. *Leading to Baptism and Church Membership*

Often the hesitant one will say, "Yes, I am willing to trust Jesus Christ as my Saviour, but why should I be baptized and join the church? Can I not be saved without this?" The answer is, "Why should you want to be saved without baptism and church membership?" Suppose someone should say, "I want to go to Europe. Do I have to take a steamship?" "No," we may reply. "You might go on a sail boat or in an airplane, but why not take the safe, regular way?" Baptism and church membership never saved anybody, but those who are saved have little excuse for disobeying Christ's plain command and refusing to become members of his body, the church, through which he proposes to carry on his work in the world. If all Christians everywhere refused to be baptized and to line up with a church, what would become of Christ's redemptive program? How would the gospel have come to any of us, had it not been through the organized efforts of faithful Christians who have constituted Christ's churches throughout the ages?

If one is a Christian, why not obey Christ in baptism and join his church? Is there anything to be gained by staying out of the church? Is there anything to be ashamed of in becoming a member of Christ's church? Ponder these words of Dr. W. W. Hamilton: "The church is not earth-born, is not of lowly origin, but is of God, is heavenly in its character. It is built upon the foundation of the Apostles, Jesus Christ himself being the chief corner-stone. It is the church of the living God, the pillar and ground of the truth, and it is the bride of the Lord Jesus Christ. It should therefore have the high place which the Saviour has given it, in our devotion and loyalty and service. The material of the church is not that of brick or stone or wood or slate or shingles. The stones are 'living,' the material spiritual, and when it is fitly framed together it grows into an holy temple in the Lord, an habitation of God through the Spirit. The blessings are so countless which Jesus bestows through the church that words fail and imagination grows weary in any attempt to enumerate or to estimate them. We, too, should hold high ideals for the work and the purity and the life of this heavenly institution."

Let us not stop short, in our soul-winning effort, of bringing the believer to decision for baptism and church membership, in obedience to the command of our Lord and Saviour, Jesus Christ.

QUESTIONS FOR REVIEW AND CLASS DISCUSSION

1. What are some of the motives that impel us in what we do? What is the Christian worker's master-motive?

2. What is the result when we link our love with God's love in winning the lost? In what sense is evangelism a divine-human partnership?

3. Give what you consider the half-dozen most necessary qualifications for becoming a skilful soul-winner.

4. What do you consider five of the most important qualifications of a good salesman? Show in a few sentences how these business principles may be applied in winning the lost to Christ and to his church.

5. What are some of the mistakes to be avoided in approaching an individual about becoming a Christian? Give briefly an example of how you would undertake to make the approach.

6. How is the Christian worker to get in touch with unsaved people who are to be won? Give a half-dozen ways in which contacts may be formed for soul-winning purposes.

7. How would you go about finding what is the real barrier between the soul and the Saviour? Who should do most of the talking? What is the danger of argument?

8. Why must the personal worker be patient and persevering? How long continue to hope and pray before giving up?

9. What shall you do when the individual agrees with you, but wants to delay decision? Why is it not wise to over-persuade?

10. Should the person with whom you are dealing accept Christ as Saviour, but object to public confession and joining the church, what would you say?

DOUBTS AND DIFFICULTIES

OUTLINE

I. DEALING WITH MASS PREJUDICE AND UNBELIEF
   1. How Deal with Those Who Are Prejudiced?
   2. How Take It When the Crowds Turn Away?

II. DEALING WITH MORAL AND RELIGIOUS DIFFICULTIES
   1. What Kind of Moral Character Does God Require?
   2. What Is the Effect of Faith in Christ on Character?
   3. What Is the Connection Between Morals and Religion?

III. DEALING WITH INTELLECTUAL DIFFICULTIES
   1. How Do We Know There Is a God?
   2. What Sort of Being Is God?
   3. Is Christianity Contrary to Science?

IV. DEALING WITH PRACTICAL DIFFICULTIES
   1. What Do I Get Out of It?
   2. What Will I Have to Give Up?
   3. What Will Happen to My Business?
   4. What Will People Say?

DOUBTS AND DIFFICULTIES

I. Dealing with Mass Prejudice and Unbelief

After nearly two thousand years the great majority of the people of the world still are without Christ. Fully half the world's population has never had a chance to believe on him, since no one has ever taken to them the saving message.

Do we sometimes grow discouraged over this mass unbelief? Does it sometimes look as if the Christian enterprise is a failure? Can we ever hope to reach and win these ignorant, prejudiced, godless masses? What attitude shall we take toward those who are governed by their prejudices, and who will not give the gospel a chance at their minds and hearts? In a day of confusion and discouragement, we need a new spirit of daring and fresh courage for the attack on the world's unbelief. We get our inspiration in this discussion from that grand old Christian warrior of old, the apostle Paul, who never knew defeat and who, almost single-handed, attacked the Roman Empire for Christ in the firm belief that Christ must someday conquer this mighty empire. Let us catch afresh something of Paul's spirit as we enter into this chapter.

1. *How Deal with Those Who Are Prejudiced?*

Prejudice is one of the greatest foes of truth. It is even worse than ignorance. Prejudice is a prejudging of the case before the facts are in. A prejudiced mind is a closed mind, and there is more hope for the most ignorant than for the man who will not open his mind to new truth. The hatred of the Jews toward Jesus, and later toward Paul and the other Christians, grew largely out of prejudice. When it was a matter of ignorance Paul often succeeded in winning his Jewish brethren to Christ; but where prejudice was deep-seated he found himself almost invariably turned aside.

How deal with those who are prejudiced? Paul did not criticize or quarrel; he did not debate or dispute. He did three things: First, "he expounded"; that is, he took the Old Testament Scriptures and explained their meaning, showing how all the Law and the Prophets led up to Christ. Second, "he testified," bearing testimony to what he himself knew and had experienced, witnessing to what Christ had done for him and for others. Third, "he persuaded," bringing to bear all the powers of his mind and heart to get his listeners to give up their prejudices, to look at Christ as he saw him, and to decide for him as he had decided. This procedure Paul followed not occasionally, nor for a little while, but "from morning till evening." Would you not like to have listened in to Paul as he dealt with these prejudiced Jews, never tiring in the face of discouragement, and never excusing himself because of the hard circumstances under which he labored? Could we do better than to follow Paul's example in dealing with prejudiced men and women in our day?

2. How Take It When the Crowds Turn Away?

Paul's preaching and teaching, as we have seen, brought a twofold result—some believed, and some believed not. Those who rejected the message turned away, hardening their hearts against the interest which they must have felt, and refusing to listen further. It is interesting to note Paul's final word to those who turned him down and rejected his gospel. He turned for consolation to the word which God had spoken to Isaiah, the prophet of old, when he called him to preach to those who would not hear. God had plainly told Isaiah that Israel would not hear, because their unbelief and sin had closed their ears to the truth which they did not *want* to hear. There was divine rebuke in Paul's speech as he applied these words to the Jews who, in prejudice and unbelief, left him. He recognized that failure to reach and win all is a part of the experience of every prophet and preacher, and that he must not give up on this account.

What did Paul do when this group of his own people left him? His parting word is significant: "Be it known therefore unto you, that the salvation of God is sent unto the Gentiles, and that they will hear it" (Acts 28: 28). When one crowd turned away from him, he found another crowd! Little did these prejudiced Jews realize that they were turning aside from their hour of destiny, and that the religious leadership of the world was being transferred to Gentile Christians.

So it is with the prejudiced and heedless crowds today who are turning away from Christ and his church. They do not know it, but they are missing their supreme opportunity. Will Christ's cause fail because of their rejection? No! God will find others who will hear and heed the gospel message. If we of the white race prove faithless in our day, who knows but that God may even now be raising up those of another race to take our place? We may fail, but God's plan of world redemption cannot fail.

II. DEALING WITH MORAL AND RELIGIOUS DIFFICULTIES

Christianity is a religion of moral goodness. Yet it clearly reveals that we are not saved by our moral goodness. The amazing claim of Christianity is that the vilest of men or women can be instantly transformed through the power of God in Christ. Yet this is not done by magic, but comes through an act of grace on God's part to which there must be a response on man's part. Salvation is from evil unto righteousness, and if the moral life is not changed there is not sufficient evidence of salvation.

Many questions are thus raised about morality and religion. What is the difference? Can there be morality without religion? Can there be religion without morality? Does one become a Christian first and then a moral man, or a moral man first and then a Christian? What is there in the Christian religion that makes one desire goodness instead of evil, and that sustains the good life in the midst of evil associations? What sort of person ought a Christian to be? Can we always tell the difference between a Christian and a non-Christian by his moral conduct? These are the questions which we cannot escape answering if we undertake to meet the moral and religious difficulties of men.

1. *What Kind of Moral Character Does God Require?*

Paul never reached the point where he thought that he measured up to Christ's standard. He frankly said that he counted not himself to have attained, but forgetting all his past achievements, and reaching forth to the things that lay ahead, he declared it his great ambition to "press toward the mark for the prize of the high calling of God in Christ Jesus" (Phil. 3: 14). It was this longing after the perfection of character which he saw in Christ that gave Paul his chief motive for living.

The development of Christlike character is not something that takes place in the moment of conversion. It is a gradual growth, like that of the seed which must first be planted, then go through the process of germination and growth, at length to bear its ripe fruit. But just as the seed will never sprout and grow unless it has in it the life germ, so character will never produce the rich fruit of Christian graces unless there is the implanted life of Christ which comes through a genuine conversion. "Christ in you," Paul says, is the "hope of glory."

If Christ be in the heart, then sin becomes hateful, selfishness odious, while the loving service of others becomes life's chief joy. A certain amount of goodness may be found in the lives of those who are not Christians, but it never has the vital quality of the Christ-filled life. Often it is a goodness that has behind it concealed selfishness, as when men are honest because it is the best policy. The goodness of the Christian is far more than morality. It is a goodness which springs up in the heart and then finds its expression in outward conduct. Often evil slips into the life of the Christian, but it brings pain and remorse, and the Christian can never be satisfied until he has got rid of that which he knows is contrary to the will of God and the purposes of Christ.

True Christian character does not consist of a long list of separate virtues, but arises out of a longing to be like Christ, to please him, to serve him, to reproduce something of the beauty of his wonderful personality. And the glorious thing is that, as Christ gradually takes possession more and more of the life, his loveliness appears as naturally as the beautiful flowers spring from good seed planted in rich soil.

2. *What Is the Effect of Faith in Christ on Character?*

Paul knew full well what had made the difference in his life. It was not his knowledge of the moral law, nor his own striving after goodness, nor the fact that he had been baptized and joined the church. It was that Christ had come into his life, and had made all things new. When those who are in doubt ask us, "What difference in my life and character will faith in Christ make?" we can point to Paul, and give our own experience.

Faith in Christ makes a difference in our attitude toward God. Instead of believing about him, we believe in him. We see revealed in Christ God's love, God's concern for our welfare, God's pity for our sinful estate, God's willingness to make the utmost sacrifice that we may be restored to fellowship with him.

Faith in Christ makes a difference in our attitude toward others. Instead of looking upon them with suspicion and jealousy, or instead of trying to get all we can out of them for ourselves, we now look at them through the eyes of Christ. We see the best in people, we try to bring the best out of people, we want to help people find joy and happiness, we want to share with them the peace and blessedness which we have found in Christ.

Faith in Christ makes a difference in our attitude toward ourselves. Self is taken out of the center and Christ put there instead. Instead of trying to get *up* ahead of others, we are willing to get *down* underneath the load of others' need. Instead of measuring success in terms of selfish gain, we measure it in terms of sacrificial service. In the words of a great Christian business man, the Christian's motto becomes, "God first, others second, self last."

The effect on character of becoming a Christian is not some mysterious thing that cannot be understood. There is mystery—the miracle of the new birth—but it is not contrary to reason. Christ is the efficient cause, and growth in Christlikeness of character is the expected effect. Let us press upon the Agrippas of today this neglected truth!

3. *What Is the Connection Between Morals and Religion?*

Morality is righteousness as it faces toward man; religion is righteousness as it faces toward God. In Christianity the two can never be separated. Jesus said, "Thou shalt love the Lord thy God . . . [and] thy neighbor." When the love of God comes into the heart, the love of man comes with it. It is impossible to be right with the sort of God that Jesus Christ revealed and at the same time be wrong with one's fellow men. Jesus used the harsh word, "hypocrite," to describe those who claim to be religious but are not moral. Is it not equally hypocritical to claim to love others while leaving God out?

The moral ideals of Christianity are the highest known to man. The moral standards of the heathen religions are far lower than the standards of Christianity. When a Christian lowers his standard to the heathen level he betrays Christ and becomes a false witness. Yet it must always be borne in mind that the Christian is not saved because he is moral; he is moral because he is saved. This is a distinction which we must never forget in dealing with those who would substitute their self-righteousness for the righteousness of God in Christ.

III. DEALING WITH INTELLECTUAL DIFFICULTIES

1. *How Do We Know There Is a God?*

The Athenians to whom Paul preached in Acts 17 did not doubt that there were gods; they did not know who nor what nor where they were. There are those today who have gone beyond the ancient Athenians in their doubt. Many are asking, "How can we know that there is a God?" They reason something like this: In the Dark Ages, before the development of science, people thought that everything strange and extraordinary was due to the direct will of God. They thought of a storm, or a flood, or an earthquake, or a fire as "an act of God." If an epidemic of disease broke out the priests called the people to the churches for mass, and all they knew to do was to pray for the abatement of the scourge. But today we know the natural causes of most of these disasters, and instead of going to God for help we take scientific measures to control conditions and bring relief. There are some things that we still do not understand, and many attribute these things to God. But as our scientific knowledge grows, shall we not discover more and more that everything has a natural cause, and thus be able to do away with the idea of God altogether? If there is a God, they argue, he must be pure spirit; and since we are flesh there is no way by which we can possibly know him. Perhaps we shall one day find that we do not need a God, and give him up altogether.

What shall we say to people who honestly doubt whether or not there is a God? A great philosopher once said, "Two things induce the soul to reverence—the starry heavens above and the moral law within." This vast physical universe, with all its law and order, could not have made itself, nor did men make it. How account for a creation without a creator? Within man is implanted the sense of right and wrong, conscience intuitively distinguishing good from evil. How could this moral quality in man be present unless there be a righteous God from whom this moral sense has come? Everywhere and in all ages the vast majority of mankind have believed in some sort of divine being. How account for a universal belief back of which is no reality? Then there are multitudes of trustworthy, sensible people who declare that they have had experiences with God. How can there be an experience with something that has no existence? Can any thinking person really believe that there is no God? We should challenge those who claim to doubt God's existence to do some honest thinking, and they will discover that it is far more difficult to do without God than to believe in him.

2. *What Sort of Being Is God?*

It is doubtful if there is a person in the world, who has thought about the matter intelligently, who does not believe that there is some kind of God. "The fool"—and the fool only—"hath said in his heart, There is no God." But men everywhere are in doubt as to what kind of being God is. What may we think about God? Is he a person, or a principle, or a power? Is he in our world, interested in what is going on among people today, or is he far removed from the affairs of men? Is everything that happens according to his will? Then how account for accidents, disease, poverty, crime, war? If God is all-wise and all-powerful, could he not prevent the misery and suffering that fill the world? If he could prevent these terrible things and does not, can we still believe that he is a God of love? These and scores of other questions contantly arise in the minds of thoughtful people concerning the nature and being of God.

Paul, in speaking to the Athenians, did not argue the existence of God. He took the fact of God for granted, as we may well take it for granted in dealing with any intelligent person. The Athenians believed that there was one supreme God, but they were sadly mistaken about the divine nature. They had made temples and shrines and images by means of which they thought to worship their gods. Paul pointed out that their idea of God was wholly unreasonable. The supreme Being who made the world and the universe cannot be confined to temples made with hands. The Giver of Life cannot be worshiped with men's hands as though he needed anything. What sort of God is he, then?

He is the Creator of man, whom he made in his own image. He has made the human family to be his children, to dwell in unity and brotherhood on the earth. He has guided the course of human history toward a goal which he has had in mind from the beginning. He is not an absentee God who made the world, put people on it, and then went off and left them. He is above and beyond the world which he has made, but he is also in his world. It is his desire that every human being should seek after and find him, for he is not far from every one of us. He is the source of life and the sustainer of life, "for in him we live, and move, and have our being." Even without the Bible one with poetic insight could say, "For we are also his offspring." (See Acts 17:24-28.)

Thus Paul disclosed that God is a personal Being, that he is the all-wise and all-powerful Creator of all things, that he loves his human children whom he created in his image, that he is in his world caring for and loving his human family, that he longs for every person in the world to know and to love him, that upon him depends the existence of every individual. What a difference it would make in the lives of men everywhere if they thus understood God!

3. *Is Christianity Contrary to Science?*

Ours is a scientific age. The scientist says, "Believe nothing that cannot be proved." The scientist, when asked if a thing is true, replies, "Try it out and see." Can the religion of Jesus Christ stand this test?

The scientific test is exactly what Jesus invites. To his first two disciples he said, "Come and see" (John 1: 39). Again he said, "Ye shall know the truth, and the truth shall make you free" (John 8:32). Paul could fearlessly say, "Prove all things; hold fast that which is good" (1 Thess. 5:21). Christianity has absolutely nothing to fear from the true scientific spirit.

Science proposes to deal with facts. Christianity rests on historical facts. There are no better established facts in all history than the facts of the Bible. The Christian bases his certainty on the facts of experience. "I *know* whom I have believed" (2 Tim. 1:12), he can say with absolute assurance. Are not the facts of peace and joy and love and goodness as really facts as the facts of nature?

To one who doubts the power of God in Christ, we simply say, "Try it and see!" Turn in sincerity from the love of sin, take God at his word, accept and obey Christ as personal Saviour, and see what happens! Could any test be fairer? Could any proposition be more reasonable? There is a great deal of false science which claims that the material is the only form of reality; but a genuine and trustworthy science recognizes that there is reality in the spiritual as well as in the physical realm. We would bring all such honest thinkers face to face with Christ, that they may learn of him the way of life now and of life everlasting.

IV. Dealing with Practical Difficulties

Becoming a Christian is often referred to as a "conversion." A *converted* person is one who has changed his course. Back of the word "conversion" is the even more significant word, "repentance." A person who has *repented* is one who has had a radical change of mind and heart.

The word emphasized throughout is "change." There are many practical difficulties in the way of making the changes required in becoming a Christian; and many changes must continue to be made as one grows in the Christian life. As we seek to win others to Christ we must deal frankly and intelligently with the necessity for these changes. In this chapter we look at some of the practical difficulties involved. We find many answers to these practical problems in the nineteenth and twentieth chapters of Acts.

1. *"What Do I Get Out of It?"*

There are some people who ask about everything, "What do I get out of it?" Self is the center of their universe. They want to turn everything that happens to their own advantage. They even include religion in their selfishness, and conclude that people are religious because of the profit in it.

There have always been quacks and fakirs ready to jump at anything that promised profit. The writer of Acts tells of certain "vagabond Jews," among them being "seven sons of one Sceva, a Jew, and chief of the priests," who saw a chance to use this miracle-working power of Paul's for their gain. (See Acts 19:13-17.) But they quickly learned that the power of Christ could not be had for selfish ends, and that it was a dangerous thing to try to get the results of Christianity without being Christian.

It is a mistake to appeal to people to become Christians for what they can get out of it. Christianity is not a religion of getting but of giving. To approach the matter from the standpoint of selfish gain is to miss the whole point of the salvation of Christ, which is a deliverance from the bondage of selfishness to the freedom of self-giving. This question as to the right over one's life—

self or Christ—must be settled at the very outset of becoming a Christian.

2. *"What Will I Have to Give Up?"*

Life quickly accumulates many things that stand between the soul and Christ. The New Testament makes it clear that the love of sin and the love of Christ cannot abide in the same heart. The religion of Jesus Christ is a religion of intelligence and honesty. Corinth was cursed with superstition and magic that passed for religion. The people had been deceived into buying expensive books which claimed to give their possessors some sort of magic power. The Ephesians, not having a true religion, had invented a false religion; and not having the Bible, had put their faith in these foolish and evil magic books. When the power of God came upon them through Paul's preaching of Christ they realized the worthlessness and evil of their books, and many saw that they must give them up. As a result, they brought their books together, made a huge bonfire, and burned them. Luke tells us that "they counted the price of them, and found it fifty thousand pieces of silver."

As soon as the claims of Christ are pressed upon the unconverted, the question arises, What must I give up? The answer is twofold: First, you must give up self, surrendering your life wholly to Christ; and, second, you must give up sin, which is anything that stands between you and Christ. This does not mean sinless perfection, but it does mean honest willingness to part with anything, no matter how precious, if it is contrary to the will of God in Christ. From the human side, it is in the making of this decision that one becomes a Christian.

3. *"What Will Happen to My Business?"*

Most people have to work for a living. To make a comfortable living is not an easy thing. Many of us know what it is to have the pressure of life grow hard upon us, with necessities to provide and bills to pay and not enough money to meet the demands. "Business is business," we grimly say, meaning that nothing must be allowed to come between us and the practical matter of money-making.

When Paul left Corinth he went to Ephesus, a famous city in Asia Minor, captial of Proconsular Asia, noted more than for anything else for its temple of Diana. One of the most profitable lines of business in Ephesus was the making of silver shrines of Diana. Faced with the choice between Christianity and their business, the silver-smiths did not hesitate. They went forth, full of wrath, to stir up the people against Paul and his gospel. We know the story of the mob which sought Paul's life, and how Paul had to leave Ephesus because of the bitterness of opposition which the business men of the city aroused.

There are forms of business which Christianity frankly undertakes to destroy. In our day it is not so much the making of heathen shrines as it is the conducting of shrines of evil-doing—establishments for the manufac-ture and sale of alcoholic liquor, palaces of prostitution, gambling dens, places of immoral amusement, crooked businesses of all sorts, temples of false worship. When Christianity makes bold to attack these evils the result is always the same—bitter denunciation and opposition. When a man who is engaged in such things is brought face to face with the claims of Christ, he is bound to ask what effect it would have on his business should he be-come a Christian. If the business is wrong, there can be but one answer: he must make it right, or give it up. There can be no compromise on this practical issue.

4. "What Will People Say?"

Public opinion is a powerful influence in all of our lives. We may declare that we do not care what people say, but deep in our hearts we know that we do care. Scorn and ridicule are often harder to face than bullets from a gun. Many men and women have been kept from

Christ by their fear of what would be said about them should they make a public profession of religion and join the church.

It takes courage for a man or a woman of mature years to come out for Christ and publicly confess him in baptism. But why should people be ashamed to be cowards in other matters, yet willing to show a "yellow streak" in religion? Christ was no coward, Paul was not "yellow," and those who follow in their train must be willing to face ridicule, misunderstanding, gossip, even slander. In dealing with people at this point, we must not hesitate to challenge them to meet the fear of public opinion with true heroism.

Christ never promised that following him would not be costly. He plainly says that those who are not willing to put him ahead of everything else and everybody else cannot be his disciples. Is not the tendency in our day to make it too cheap and easy to be a Christian? As to the question, What will it cost me to be a Christian? the answer is, It will cost you your life! As someone has well said, "It does not take much of a man to be a Christian, but it takes all there is of him." It is only in thus losing one's life that it can be found.

QUESTIONS FOR REVIEW AND CLASS DISCUSSION

1. Is the Christian religion, on the whole, winning or losing in our day? Give two reasons for encouragement and two reasons for discouragement.

2. What is "prejudice"? What are some of the ways in which people today are prejudiced against Baptists and their message? How deal with those who are prejudiced?

3. Where do the worldly crowds flock? What attitude shall we take toward those who heedlessly refuse to give any attention to God's day, God's house, God's love, Christ's message?

4. What chief sins in our age stand between men and Christ? What is our message to those who would like to enjoy their sins and the benefits of Christianity at the same time?

5. Can one be moral without being a Christian? Can one be a Christian without being moral? Show the connection between morals and religion.

6. Suppose one with whom you are dealing should express doubt of God's existence. How would you undertake to prove that there is a God? What sort of God would you show him to be?

7. Suppose the argument should be made that Christianity is contrary to science. How would you demonstrate that the truths of religion and the truths of science cannot disagree?

8. List three or four practical difficulties that come between men and Christ. State in a few words how these difficulties are to be overcome.

9. Which are harder to meet—prejudicial, intellectual, moral, or practical difficulties? To what extent do unsaved people today have all four kinds of problems?

10. How may the Christian worker best prepare himself to deal with the many forms of doubt and difficulty that keep people from Christ today?

BY ALL MEANS WINNING ALL

OUTLINE

I. THE NEED OF REVIVAL SEASONS
1. All Life Demands Seasons of Renewal
2. The Kind of Spiritual Revival Needed Today

II. THE RELATION OF EDUCATION AND EVANGELISM
1. The Element of Learning in Salvation
2. When Education and Evangelism Are Separated
3. When Education and Evangelism Are United

III. THE SUNDAY SCHOOL AS A SOUL-WINNING AGENCY
1. The Best Soul-Winning Opportunity
2. The Best Soul-Winners

IV. THE TRAINING UNION AS A SOUL-WINNING AGENCY
1. The Training Union's Purpose—To Develop Efficient Church Members
2. Efficient Church Members Are Soul-Winners

V. TRAINING OF SOUL-WINNING MINISTERS
1. Christ's First Training School
2. Sharing in the Training of These Men

VI. WINNING THE CHILDREN
1. We Must Recognize the Child's Need of a Saviour
2. We Must Lead the Child To Confess and Follow Christ

VII. WINNING THE YOUNG PEOPLE
1. Youth, a Period of Crisis
2. The Supreme Urgency of the Task

VIII. WINNING ADULTS
1. Presenting Christ to Adults
2. Now or Never!

BY ALL MEANS WINNING ALL

When Jesus sent forth the seventy, he sent them "two by two." There was divine wisdom in this arrangement. We work best for Christ when we work with others. One person by himself will not ordinarily win many people to Christ. One church by itself is not likely to be a great soul-winning church. A group of churches with no wider fellowship will find it hard to sustain spiritual enthusiasm. Thus we follow a law of spiritual effectiveness when two people team together in soul-winning, when a group of people associate themselves together in a church, when churches reinforce themselves in a district association, when district associations ally themselves as a general association or state convention, and when all the states of the South co-operate in the Southern Baptist Convention.

I. THE NEED OF REVIVAL SEASONS

1. *All Life Demands Seasons of Renewal*

During the winter trees shed their leaves, flowers wither and die, grass becomes brown and sere, and for a time it may look as if death has laid its blighting hand on all of nature. Then one day the birds begin to return from their southern retreat, the trees begin to put out their buds, the flowers begin to grow and give promise of blossoming again, and the grass takes on its accustomed hue of green. What is happening? Why, spring is on its way again! The warmth of the sun and the moisture of the soil begin their glorious work of revival at the roots of the trees and the flowers and the grass. A strange urge lays hold of the birds in their winter home in the far south, reviving their desire to fly back to their northern homes. We thank God for the power of revival which he has implanted in all living things.

2. *The Kind of Spiritual Revival Needed Today*

An objection raised by some thoughtful Christian to the revival is that it often sweeps into the church numbers of people who are not assimilated into the church's membership and who often amount to nothing in service and usefulness. Then there is the objection that the revival is frequently followed by a reaction which leaves the church colder and less healthy than it was before the revival was held. Still another objection is that people will come to the revival day after day, get an overdose of religion, and then drop out until the next revival a year later. Sometimes the people of the world accuse us of having a "chills and fever" type of religion—an eleven months' chill in which we take our religion very lightly, and then an annual monthly fever of unnatural religious excitement.

We are bound to confess that some types of evangelistic meetings have their dangers. There can be the wrong sort as well as the right sort. But is not this true of everything? What sort of revival is needed in our churches today?

First, the revival should be true to its plain meaning—the reawakening of interest and devotion on the part of Christian people themselves. The starting place of the revival most needed today is in the hearts and lives of professing Christians.

Second, the needed revival is one in which there is a large element of teaching. We deeply need a revival of understanding and appreciation of the great doctrines of grace which lie at the foundation of our religion. Intelligent instruction should precede appeal to emotion.

Third, we need a revival which will result in reconsecration to Christ and to his purposes for us as Christians. Too many Christians are resting on an experience that has grown cold and lifeless. They are saying, "once saved, always saved," and, resting on this assurance, they have given up prayer, Bible study, meditation, sacrificial service. There is vast need in all our churches for a new and living dedication of all that we are and have to Christ and to his redemptive program for the human family.

Fourth, we need a revival of love not only to Christ but also to one another. Christ's supreme command is that we as Christians love one another. John's test of salvation is simply this: "We know that we have passed from death unto life, because we love the brethren. He that loveth not his brother abideth in death" (1 John 3:14). In many of our churches there is too much coldness and even bitterness among Christian people themselves. No great spiritual movement may be expected in a church until this barrier is broken down.

Fifth, we need a revival of compassion and concern for the lost. The simple truth is that many Christians have apparently ceased to care for the souls of the unsaved. For their own sake as well as for the sake of a lost world they need to have their hearts burdened afresh for those who are without Christ and for whom Christ died. What a new day would dawn for any church if its members—not just a few, but all—could be led to accept their responsibility for the lost and to become so burdened for their salvation that they could have no peace until they saw the unsaved being converted!

II. THE RELATION OF EDUCATION AND EVANGELISM

1. *The Element of Learning in Salvation*

While we are not saved by what we know, knowledge does play a real part in our salvation. If one knew nothing whatever of Jesus Christ, could he be saved? The first step in salvation is repentance of sin, but could one repent of sin who had never learned the meaning of sin and its consequences? In salvation repentance must be accompanied by faith, but could one have faith in a Christ of whom he had never heard and in a gospel of which he was totally ignorant? Knowledge is not salvation, but it is a means used of the Holy Spirit to bring salvation. Christ alone saves, but connection must be made between Christ and the sinner, and this connection comes through knowledge.

There is no point in the Christian life at which knowledge does not play some part. The proof of salvation is obedience, but how can one obey the commandments of Christ when those commandments are unknown? The expression of the Christian life is unselfish service, but how can one serve who knows nothing about how to serve? The Christian life is nourished by prayer and worship, but how can one pray and worship aright who has never learned the meaning of these acts? The Bible is the Christian's guidebook, but how can one be guided by a book which he has never studied?

2. When Education and Evangelism Are Separated

Suppose a church should say, "Our supreme business is winning souls to Christ. Let the schools educate; that is their business." What would be the result? Emotional evangelism without education might create a great stir and get people excited about their spiritual condition; but would it truly win souls to Christ if "accepting Christ" meant only an emotional upsetting? There have been evangelistic meetings in which people were stirred to make a profession of religion without being taught the meaning and obligations of the Christian life. It is a sad fact that many of those who thus join the church soon drift away, some of them becoming more hardened to the claims of Christ than if they had never made a profession.

Churches that major on evangelism apart from Christian education may have a mushroom growth, but they rarely become permanently strong and useful. Untaught Christians are not apt to be strong in Christian character, generous in giving, nor missionary in purpose. A church that stresses evangelism without education is like a man trying to walk on one leg. He may hop about, and create a great deal of noise, and put forth a great amount of energy, but he will not make much progress on a long journey. A church depending upon evangelism without education is a crippled church.

3. *When Education and Evangelism Are United*

Suppose a church should go to the other extreme and say, "Our supreme business is to educate; let others evangelize." The result would be slow but certain spiritual death. As a matter of fact, there is no true Christian education that leaves out evangelism. A part of the educative process is to teach people the meaning of sin and repentance, to lead them to love and trust Jesus Christ, and to show them how to obey him in confession and service. It is foolish to put evangelism over against Christian education as if they were opposites. Evangelism is the end, Christian education is the means; saved souls are the fruit, Christian nurture is the cultivation of the soil, the sowing of the seed, and the gathering of the fruit. The best evangelistic preaching has in it the teaching element; and the best Christian teaching has in it the evangelistic note. As well try to separate the seed from the soil and expect a crop as to separate evangelism from Christian education and expect a gospel harvest. Where Christian education has done its work well evangelism is made easier and its results more permanent. Where the motive of evangelism has been uppermost Christian education has been made warm, sound, fruitful, and abiding.

Here are some words from a thoughtful writer which we would do well to ponder: "Educational evangelism holds that the gospel is not simply a message to men but a power to generate righteousness in their souls and develop godliness from within; seeks not merely to tell men of Christ, but to build Christ himself—his consciousness of God, his union with the will of God—into the personality of men . . . This is an ideal, at once of evangelism and of religious education, which Jesus set forth in his practice, which the scientific interpretation of the nature of the soul and the meaning of the gospel for it supports, and which the church is coming in our time more clearly to see, and more widely, deliberately, and joyfully to accept."[1]

III. THE SUNDAY SCHOOL AS A SOUL-WINNING AGENCY

It is a well known fact that the great majority of additions to our churches by baptism come through the Sunday school. It has been estimated that eighty-five out of every one hundred who join our churches have been reached first through the Sunday school, and led from Sunday school membership to church membership. If this is only approximately correct, it puts a tremendous premium on the Sunday school as an evangelistic agency. If, in a great department store, it were discovered that three-fourths of the new customers were being secured through the attractiveness and service of one department, would not wise management insist upon developing that department to its utmost efficiency? The Sunday school should not overshadow other departments of the church, and Sunday school officers and teachers must always recognize that their success depends upon the work of other departments and the church as a whole. Yet wisdom demands that the Sunday school be magnified as the greatest outreaching and ingathering agency which we possess in modern church life. It is timely, when we are seeking an awakening of interest in evangelism everywhere, to focus attention upon the Sunday school as a God-given means for winning the lost to Christ and adding them to his church.

1. *The Best Soul-Winning Opportunity*

In this great matter of soul-winning the Sunday school teacher has an advantage over the preacher. The preacher delivers his message to a mixed congregation,

---

[1]McKinley, Charles E., *Educational Evangelism*, p. 122. Now out of print.

made up of many ages and many levels of experience and need. As a rule, people do not interrupt the preacher to ask questions if they do not understand his message, nor does he question his hearers, one by one, to discover their difficulties and points of view. The Sunday school teacher has a relatively small group of boys or girls, or men or women, of approximately the same age. The teacher can ask and answer questions, and thus can meet individual needs as they arise. The close personal touch gives the teacher opportunity to know intimately the lives of his students, and so he can present the claims of Christ to each one in the way that will be most convincing. If a Sunday school teacher is not a soul-winner it is not because of lack of opportunity.

The pastor and the Sunday school teacher should work together in the winning of Sunday school pupils to Christ. Dr. Burroughs, in his book, *Winning to Christ,* tells of a discouraged teacher who came to her pastor expressing the wish to give up her class, saying, "I seem unable to win my girls to the Saviour." The pastor said, "Let us try one time more. Invite two of the girls to your home tomorrow, and I will drop in and talk the matter over with them." The next afternoon the pastor came into the teacher's home and found two bright girls seated there. He opened the great subject of salvation immediately and presented the claims of Jesus. There in "teacher's home" the two girls gave their hearts to the Saviour. Within a week every lost girl in the class had been invited to the home of the teacher and had there confessed Jesus. Would it not be glorious if every Sunday school teacher and every pastor should thus work together in seizing this greatest of all opportunities for the winning of lost boys and girls?

2. The Best Soul-Winners

Who are the soul-winning Christians in almost any church? With rare exceptions, they are the Sunday school teachers and officers, and the active workers in

---

*Now out of print.

the Sunday school departments and classes. Go to any church and ask the pastor for a list of the people who can be depended upon to do personal work, and you may be sure that the large majority of those listed will be active workers in the Sunday school.

If there is a teacher in a Sunday school anywhere who is not a soul-winning Christian, that teacher should search his heart to know the reason. To teach without leading unsaved members of the class toward and to Christ would be like a farmer planting seed but failing to harvest the crop. If there are no unsaved members of the class, then the class should be led by the teacher to go out into the highways and hedges to seek and to save the lost where they are. If the class is made up of little children too young to accept Christ, the teacher should be leading them toward Christ so that they will accept him as soon as they reach the age of accountability; and unsaved fathers and mothers of these little ones should be sought and won. Is there any excuse whatever for a Sunday school teacher going an entire year without having led someone to the Saviour?

IV. The Training Union as a Soul-Winning Agency

1. *The Training Union's Purpose—To Develop Efficient Church Members*

What did your church do for you the first few months after you were baptized to help you become a happy, fruitful Christian and a competent, useful church member? Some of the older ones of us would have to reply, "Nothing." For there was a time in our churches when practically no opportunity was offered the young Christian for development in those graces and abilities which are necessary to an efficient church member.

It has been less than fifty years since our Baptist churches worked out a successful plan for training in church membership. At first this organization was called the Baptist Young People's Union, and consisted of a group of young people who met for purposes of prayer, Bible study, mission study, and the deepening of their spiritual lives. Gradually the scope of the Baptist Young People's union enlarged to take in the Intermediate age, then the Juniors, and at length the Adults. With the addition of a Story Hour for little children, a graded training service was made complete, and the name Baptist Training Union adopted.

At the head of the list of those skills which the Training Union seeks to develop is ability to witness for Christ so effectively that others will accept him. Programs, study courses, Bible readings, prayer, and practical soul-winning activities combine to make the Training Union one of the most powerful of modern evangelistic forces. Each church should utilize its Training Union to its fullest capacity in this twofold way—as a school for the development of all its members, and as a force for winning the lost.

2. *Efficient Church Members Are Soul-Winners*

Suppose in a business organization the manager should call together his salesmen and say to them, "The most important thing that I have for you to do is to go out and tell others about our business and win new customers." Suppose fifteen out of eighteen of the members of this business organization should draw back and refuse to do their part. It is clear that the business would be a relative failure unless the manager could somehow persuade the shirkers to get in line, or else get others to take their places.

The church of Jesus Christ is in the greatest business on earth. Its members are all salesmen, responsible under the orders of their great Head, Jesus Christ, to go forth and tell others of his salvation, persuade them to accept it, and enlist them in the work of going out and winning others. It was never intended that one-sixth of the church members should do all the witnessing. If a church would be at its best it must enlist the other five-sixths in this main business for which it exists, and then teach and train them so that they can be successful "salesmen" for Christ and his church. Can anyone be thought of as a good church member who goes year after year without doing the one main thing which Christ has commanded every church member to do? No church will ever be the church it ought to be until many more of its members are led to see this truth and are enlisted as active personal soul-winners

V. THE TRAINING OF SOUL-WINNING MINISTERS

1. *Christ's First Training School*

Christ came into the world to seek and to save a lost humanity. He had in his heart the whole human race, including the millions who were then living and the uncounted billions who have lived from that time until now. Yet coming to live and to die for these vast multitudes, he chose a dozen men through whom to inaugurate his redemptive plan. He spent more time teaching and training these twelve men than in anything else to which he gave himself while he was on earth. These men he called his apostles, or missionaries, whom he ordained "that they should be with him, and that he might send them forth to preach, and to have power to heal sicknesses, and to cast out devils" (Mark 3:14-15).

Never were the demands made upon the minister more varied and more difficult than today. Can we expect any man to fulfil these demands without thorough training? This training he may get from private study and personal experience, but it stands to reason that his qualifications will be more quickly acquired if he goes to a school which specializes in the training of ministers.

2. *Sharing in the Training of These Men*

There are, on the average, about twelve hundred young men and women in the several Southern Baptist training camps for ministers and missionaries. God

has called them, Christ has ordained them, the Holy
Spirit is empowering them. Most of them cannot go to
school and make a living at the same time. They are
matching their lives against our money! Shall we ask
them to do all the sacrificing? Or shall we help them
to secure their training, and then go to the fields where
the Lord wants them and where they are so sorely
needed? In order that they may do their part, we must
do our part. Could any investment bring richer divi-
dends through time and eternity than a bit of money
invested in the lives of these consecrated servants of
Christ?

VI. WINNING THE CHILDREN

1. *We Must Recognize the Child's Need of a Saviour*

Jesus did not say, "Bring babies to me and baptize
them in my name." He said, "Suffer the little children
to *come* unto me." How old must a child be before he
can *come* to Christ? Well, that depends. Some children
develop more rapidly than others. Some are more spiritually sensitive than others. Some have a better background of teaching than others. A child is old enough
to come to Christ (1) when he is old enough to realize
that he has committed sin, and (2) when he is old
enough to turn away from the love of sin and turn in
faith and love to Christ as personal Saviour.

Some people argue that the child should be let alone
until he is old enough to make his own unaided choice.
It is said that on one occasion an English statesman
declared in the presence of Coleridge, the Christian poet,
that a child should wait until he is grown and then choose
his own religion. Coleridge made no reply, but led the
speaker out into his garden. Looking around the bare
ground he said quietly: "I have decided not to put
out any flowers and vegetables this year, but wait till
August and let the garden decide for itself whether it
prefers weeds or strawberries!" What shall one do to

raise a crop of weeds? Why, nothing at all! What shall a child do to be lost? Why, nothing at all! The seed of sin is in the child's nature by birth, and needs only time and occasion to bring forth its fruit of disobedience and death.

Let us make no mistake about it: the child becomes a sinner as soon as he consciously does wrong; and as soon as he becomes a sinner he needs a Saviour. We may let the child alone, but we may be perfectly sure that the devil will not. It is of utmost importance that the child be led early to see his need of Christ as Saviour, and this is the sacred duty of parents, teachers pastors.

2. We Must Lead the Child to Confess and Follow Christ

It is not enough to induce a child to say that he accepts Christ and wants to join the church because we want him to do it. One of the gravest sins that could be committed against the child is to lead him into joining the church without having had a personal experience of conversion. The child should not be led merely to repeat words after us, the meaning of which he does not understand. Nor should he be permitted to join the church just because others are joining. With utmost care the child should be led to make his own decision, realizing that it is not an easy thing to live the Christian life, and that there are obligations of church membership which must be assumed honestly and intelligently. On the one hand is the danger of interfering with the child's religious expression, standing between him and Christ because we do not think the child is old enough to know what he is doing. On the other hand is the equally disastrous mistake of overpersuading children to make a profession of faith which has little or no meaning for them, and which they afterwards deny.

Every child, before being received for baptism, should be carefully questioned in private to see whether or not he really has had an experience of grace. This does not mean that the child must pass a theological examination, for there are many things about the Bible and Christianity which he cannot be expected yet to know. If a spiritual awakening has come to the child, this is the time of all times to clear up his misunderstandings, and to lead him to a true experience of repentance and faith. But if the child has not the root of the matter in him, if he has no consciousness of sin and no felt need of a Saviour, if Christ is just a name to him and he wants to be baptized and to join the church in order to allay his childish fears of being lost or in order to "be good," baptism by all means should be delayed until these errors are cleared away and the child is ready in mind and in heart for this public witness of his death to a life of sin, his burial with Christ, and his rising to walk in a new life.

VII. WINNING THE YOUNG PEOPLE

1. *Youth, a Period of Crisis*

As we grow older, are we not inclined to forget when we were young? About the age of thirteen or fourteen the normal person awakes to the fact that he is no longer a child. He finds himself in possession of the powers of a man, yet he has only the experiences of a child. We call these years from thirteen to sixteen the "intermediate" years, since they stand in between childhood and maturity. During these years boys and girls are "getting their growth." Physically, growth is very rapid, resulting in awkwardness, uncertainty, self-consciousness. Nature is making such heavy demands of growth that it takes a great deal of food and rest to supply the demand.

Mentally, a new world opens up. The boy or girl passes to high school, and begins to get acquainted with many ideas which are strange and upsetting. Socially, it is a time of adjustment. Boys and girls become conscious of each other, new acquaintances and companionships are formed, and there is a constant craving for amusement and excitement. Spiritually, it is a time of crisis. Boys and girls come during these years to a full realization of the meaning of sin, and begin to make choices that will last for life. These are the years when more people accept Christ and join the church than at any other age; and it is during these years that more boys and girls enter upon careers of sin and crime than at any other stage of life.

The intermediate years are years of change and adjustment; the young people's age that follows—from seventeen to about twenty-five—is a time of settling into the moulds which will shape adulthood. What young people become from seventeen to twenty-five they will remain, in many respects, the rest of their lives. During this period they decide their life work, they make their choice of life companions, they choose the social circle in which they will move, they lay the foundations of future business success or failure, they adopt the moral principles which will guide their lives. During these critical years the majority make their final decision for or against Christ, and either find their places happily in the church or turn aside from the church to the things of the world.

Do we not see afresh how supremely important it is that we do our utmost to help these young people meet the crisis which they confront during these meaningful years so that they will give their lives whole-heartedly to Christ and to his church? Can anything compensate for our failure to reach these young people for Christ during this formative period? If we fail here, the failure will follow us and them through eternity.

2. *The Supreme Urgency of the Task*

Other things may wait, but the winning of our young people to Christ is something that must not be put off. Delay is not only dangerous; it is often fatal. If we let these young people slip through our fingers, and go out into the world without Christ, many of them will go out into a Christless eternity.

Here, as one thoughtful writer has recently put it, is youth's call to us: "This is our task, a sacred task, and worthy of the best we can give it. We must not forget either that it is youth that has the greater stakes in the ultimate issue. And youth at heart is sound. Nor will youth refuse us its co-operation and support. In spite of the silly clamor of those who would have us believe that modern youth has unaccountably been endowed with some superhuman sense which gives it access to all the realms of wisdom denied in the past, and renders it immune to moral poisons, which, from the dawn of history, have worked their ills on humankind, youth still looks to those of age and experience to guide it in ways that human experience has proved to be wise and safe. And youth has no gratitude in its heart for those who, in the pursuit of their own selfish pleasures, have neglected the greater and more sacred task, for the lack of which the solid satisfactions that properly belong to the years of maturity must ever be denied.

"Youth has still its God-given visions of what life can and should be. Only as it realizes these visions in its later years will it find life rich and full and free; and experience teaches us only too plainly that youth must have the help of its elders if it is to reach the high goal that these visions challenged it to seek."

VIII. WINNING ADULTS

In every community there will be found a considerable number of grown men and women who have never made a profession of faith in Christ and joined his church. With some it is a matter of neglect and delay. Others have grown "gospel-hardened." Still others have deliberately rejected Christ and are living lives of open sin. A few are skeptics and atheists, claiming that they do not believe in the Bible, in God, or in Christ. Some are comparatively young, and are wrapped up in their own affairs. Some have reached middle life, and are "set in their ways." Others are getting old, and must soon face the judgment without Christ and without hope. What should be our attitude toward these unsaved adults? How may we work together to win them to Christ? What shall we do about the backslidden church members who are sometimes even harder to reach than those who have never made a profession of religion? These are questions which call for our best and most earnest thought.

1. *Presenting Christ to Adults*

How shall we present Christ to our unsaved adult friends? There is no cut-and-dried procedure, but the following are some suggestions that have been found helpful:

(1) Know Christ yourself, and love him devotedly.

(2) Know Christ's simple plan of salvation—repentance, faith, confession, obedience, service.

(3) Know human nature, and love the souls of lost men and women.

(4) Win the confidence of the one whom you would bring to Christ.

(5) Don't argue; just tell what Christ has done for you, and read his own words in which he tells what he will do for anyone who trusts him.

(6) Be patient with doubts and difficulties; don't hurry, but don't be too easily put off.

(7) Get at the real root of the trouble—sin—and show how Christ's atoning death is the only remedy for sin.

(8) Pray much, and lean hard on the Holy Spirit for guidance.

(9) Lead from the private confession of Christ to the duty and privilege of public profession in baptism and church membership.

2. *Now or Never!*

Life insurance statistics place the average span of life today at about sixty-five years. Some will die earlier and some later than this, but the average holds good. Has it fully dawned upon you that the middle-aged men and women of your acquaintance have just a few years more to live? Think of those forty years old and beyond who have passed away during the recent years. How unspeakably dangerous it is for men and women at this time of life to go on risking a Christless eternity!

If any one of us passed by a house late at night in which we knew that a friend was sleeping, and saw that house on fire, what would we do? Without a moment's hesitation we would disturb this friend's slumber, and rescue him if possible from his danger. Yet there are all around us men and women who will soon be in the grave, but who are unaware of their terrible danger of dying unsaved. Ought we not to be even more concerned for the safety of their souls than their bodies? It may be that within the next month some unsaved friend will pass from time to eternity to be forever lost unless some one of us bears faithful witness for Christ and wins this lost one to the Saviour. May we not put it off, but go even now, as John and Andrew went to James and Peter, that we may bring these precious souls to the Saviour while there is yet time!

QUESTIONS FOR REVIEW AND CLASS DISCUSSION

1. Why are revival seasons necessary in the spiritual realm as in the physical? What would be the result if our churches ceased to hold revival meetings?

2. In answer to the question, What kind of revival do we need? List five marks of the sort of revival you would like to see come to your church.

3. Suppose there should arise a contention in your church, some saying, "What we need is not education but evangelism," while others insist, "What we need is not evangelism but Christian education." Give your argument as to why *both* are necessary.

4. What are the advantages of the Sunday school which make it the most efficient soul-winning agency of the church? Give at least five suggestions as to how your Sunday school may be made more effective in its work of educational evangelism.

5. What twofold part should the Baptist Training Union play in the church's evangelistic program? How can your Training Union be made more fruitful for evangelism?

6. Why are so many church members unenlisted in this main business for which Christ has saved them? Make at least three practical suggestions as to how more members of your church can be induced to personal witnessing.

7. Ministers must train their members as soul-winners. Tell briefly how church members may share in the training of soul-winning ministers.

8. When is a child old enough to be won to Christ? What two contrasting mistakes should be avoided? Tell in a few words how you would go about winning a child to the Saviour.

9. Why is it supremely important to win Intermediates and young people? What is the danger if they pass into adulthood unsaved? Tell how you would go about the winning of an unsaved young person.

10. Why is it so difficult to win adults to Christ? Give five of the most valuable suggestions as to how to present Christ to adults.

UNTO THE UTTERMOST

OUTLINE

I. SALVATION FOR THE WORST OF MEN
  1. The Helpless and Despised
  2. Those Who Put Money Ahead of Christ
  3. The Overcoming Power of Love

II. SALVATION FOR THE WHOLE OF LIFE
  1. Salvation Includes the Physical Life
  2. Salvation Includes the Mental Life
  3. Salvation Includes the Social Life
  4. Salvation of the Soul Is All-Inclusive

III. SALVATION FOR TIME AND ETERNITY
  1. We Are NOW the Children of God
  2. We Are NOW Freed from the Curse of Sin
  3. We Are NOW To Live the Saved Life
  4. Eternity Is NOW in Our Hearts

IV. SALVATION FOR ALL MEN EVERYWHERE
  1. The Shadow That Falls Across the World
  2. The Promise of a Glorious Dawn
  3. Light for All Who Sit in Darkness

UNTO THE UTTERMOST

Christianity is a religion of superlatives. It proposes to go unto the uttermost parts of the earth with salvation unto the uttermost for the worst of men and the whole of life for eternity. In this chapter we join evangelism and missions in holy union for worldwide ends.

I. Salvation for the Worst of Men

If we were to make a list of all the lost people in our church community, no doubt we would check some of them off as "hopeless cases." For one reason or another we would feel that it was useless to go to them with the gospel message. Are we justified in looking upon any human being as a "hopeless case"? True, Jesus himself did not win all to whom he appealed; but the ones that he failed to win we might have thought of as most hopeful, while some of those whom he won we would no doubt have put in our "hopeless" list. We would have expected him to win the Jewish religious leaders, the young Jewish rulers, the pious Jewish people; yet they turned him down and finally crucified him. Who would have expected him to win the Samaritan woman and her neighbors, the lepers and the beggars, the publicans and crooks, the despised and outcast? Yet many of these accepted him and were gloriously saved.

Does not all this go to prove that while there may be "hopeless" cases, we have no way of knowing who they are, and so should never pronounce judgment? There is a verse of an old song which says, "While the light holds out to burn, the vilest sinner may return." May our hearts be stirred to fresh faith as we look at the amazing truth that there is salvation through Christ for the worst of men.

1. *The Helpless and Despised*

Take the case of Jerry McAuley. He had been a prisoner at Sing Sing, where he came under the influence of the gospel and was converted. He was pardoned, but found himself friendless and an outcast. The thirst for liquor overcame him, and one day he lay drunk outside a saloon in Water Street, one of the wickedest sections of New York. A city missionary, Mr. Little, was giving out tracts, and Jerry McAuley, in his drunken stupor, heard the missionary speak of Jesus. The poor fellow managed to pull himself together, and entered into conversation with Mr. Little. This good man of God took Jerry McAuley in hand, and although Jerry slipped many times his friend would not give him up, until at last the missionary's love and the power of Christ enabled Jerry to conquer his appetite for drink and become a sober and self-respecting man. Later McAuley established the Water Street Mission, and became one of the most successful soul-winners of his generation. Thousands of broken-down bums were rescued through his untiring work, led to Christ, and made over into good citizens. Here again we find living witness to the truth that there is salvation through Christ for the worst of men.

Are we not in danger, with all our church respectability, of losing sight of the helpless and despised, the blind beggars and the Jerry McAuleys? It was for such as these that Christ came, and it is to such as these that he would send us with his message of redeeming love. It is a sad day for any Christian, and for any church, when the love of wrecked and ruined men is lost, and faith in the power of Christ to save them is given up.

2. *Those Who Put Money Ahead of Christ*

In the tenth chapter of Mark we find another type of lost individual. We see a young man, wealthy and distinguished, coming to Jesus with the question, "Good Master, what shall I do to inherit eternal life?" The young man acknowledged Jesus as a great teacher, but evidently he was not thinking of him as a divine Saviour. "Why callest thou me good?" Jesus asked. "None is good, save one, that is, God." In this way Jesus challenged the young man to think of him as more than a great human teacher. Then he began probing the young ruler further. Measured by the standard of morality the young man stood the test well. Then Jesus put his finger on the sore spot: "Yet lackest thou one thing: Sell all that thou hast, and distribute unto the poor, and thou shalt have treasure in heaven: and come, follow me." In one sentence the result is simply told: "And he was sad at this saying, and went away grieved: for he had great possessions." (Luke 18:22.)

What was this barrier between the young man and Christ? Evidently it was his love of money. Jesus claimed the mastery over his life. Money claimed the mastery. The young man cast the deciding vote, and money won. So far as we know, this splendid young man, with all his advantages and moral character, proved a "hopeless case." He became a living illustration of the Pharisee in the parable which Jesus had just given.

Over against this wealthy and privileged kind of sinner put Harold Begbie's story of "Old Born Drunk." Old Born Drunk was the product of the slums of London. He was the child of frightfully drunken parents, had been born in drink, and was almost certainly, as his name declared, actually born drunk. He had been taught to drink from babyhood, and at the age of forty-five was a stupid drunkard. A Salvation Army girl found him in the filthy den where he lived, and at last induced him to attend the meeting and come forward for prayer. Then the miracle took place, and Old Born Drunk was converted. Years followed, and not once did he touch liquor again. When he died he was buried with military honors, and thousands of people lined the streets and followed the procession to the cemetery. His story is a living witness to the truth that there is salvation for the worst of men. Do we believe this as we ought?

3. *The Overcoming Power of Love*

What is it that reaches these hard cases, breaks down their resistance, and brings them to the new life in Christ? It is not rebuke, nor pity, nor argument, but *love*. First, there must be genuine love in our hearts for them. Then there must be revealed to them the love of God in Christ, so that they see God as a loving Father yearning over them that they may have eternal life. To our love and the love of God in Christ they must somehow be led to respond with a like love, and in the softening of their hearts the Holy Spirit will find opportunity to plant the truth which will bring forth the fruit of salvation.

When the critics of Jesus murmured against him because he went to be the guest of Zaccheus, the "publican and sinner," Jesus pointed to the converted man, saying, "For the Son of man is come to seek and to save that which is lost" (Luke 19:10). Have we forgotten that this is the mission of our Master, and that it must be our mission if we are true to him?

II. SALVATION FOR THE WHOLE OF LIFE

Our lives are not made up of water-tight compartments. Our bodies are closely related to our souls. Body and spirit are greatly influenced by the people with whom we live. If the physical life, or the mental life, or the social life, or the spiritual life go wrong the whole life is affected. Christ came to be the Saviour of the whole life. Do we not sometimes mistakenly think that Christ's only concern is for the soul, and that religion has nothing to do with the saving of the body, and of the life among men? A study of Christ's work while he was on earth will show that he healed sick bodies, he restored crazed minds, he made people right with one another, and he regenerated lost souls.

A full and complete evangelism calls for the surrender of all of life to Christ, and promises his salvation for the whole of life. It is a one-sided gospel message that puts all the emphasis on physical healing, or on mental healing, or on social service, or on the soul apart from everyday living. A full salvation involves (1) the sanctifying of our bodies, (2) the consecration of our minds, (3) the Christianizing of our social relationships, and (4) eternal life with Christ.

1. *Salvation Includes the Physical Life*

In the twelfth chapter of Romans, which has been called "the Christian's code," Paul sets forth the fulness of salvation which Christ has brought. He begins, as Christ began, with the body. He has just completed his great argument, showing that God's promise has not failed concerning Israel, but that the new Israel are those who have been redeemed by Christ. The Jews, through their sin and unbelief, had ceased to be the true Israel, and their place was now being taken by the chosen in Christ. What sort of people, then, ought God's redeemed to be? With passionate earnestness Paul pours out his heart to us in the entreaty that we accept Christ's full salvation and measure up at every point to God's stand- ard for his new chosen people. His very first word concerns the physical life: "I beseech you therefore, brethren, by the mercies of God, that ye present *your bodies* a living sacrifice, holy, acceptable unto God, which is your reasonable service" (Rom. 12:1).

We cannot do without our bodies, but what shall we do with them? Paul gives us the secret when he says, "Present your bodies a living sacrifice, holy, acceptable unto God, which is your reasonable service." When the body is wholly surrendered to God, so that Christ is Lord of the physical life, two things happen: Victory is won over the temptations of the flesh, and power is given to make the body the servant of God and of the higher things of the Spirit. It does not always follow that disease and handicaps will disappear, but often the causes of illness and weakness will be removed and thus health restored; and even though this be not the case,

Christ's grace will prove sufficient, and in spite of the physical difficulty there may be a life of great joy and usefulness. Ought we not to make more of Christ's great doctrine of health, and show to sinful, suffering people how he is the Saviour of the body?

2. *Salvation Includes the Mental Life*

Jesus dealt first with the body, but he did so in order that he might reach the mind. His appeal was to intelligence. He knew all about those whose minds had gone wrong, and his love went out to them in their restoration to sanity. He drove out the evil spirits which had taken possession of men's minds, so that the disordered mental life could become normal. We think at once of the devil cast out of the dumb man (Matt. 9:32, 33); of the woman of Canaan whose daughter was "grievously vexed with a devil" (Matt. 15:22); of the wild maniac of Gadara (Luke 8:26-36); of the epileptic boy whom the disciples could not heal (Luke 9:38-42). Nowhere is the divine power of Christ made more real than in his mastery of the evil forces that come in and take possession of people's minds. He entered into a realm where none but God can command, and dealt with those mysterious enemies that upset men's minds, bringing upon them all the ills that grow out of mental maladies.

The world is full of people whose minds are disordered. Insanity is increasing at an appalling rate. We are told that more people are now confined to mental hospitals than are being cared for in general hospitals. Men and women by the thousands are breaking down under the strain of modern life, and are falling victims to the evil spirits that distort their minds. Suspicion, fear, hate, covetousness, impurity, selfishness, and a great horde of devils like unto them, beset the minds of men all over the world. Is it any wonder that their minds break down, and their lives become filled with dark and ugly shadows?

Thoughtful medical men are recognizing more and more the connection between mental disease and physical disease. Christian doctors recognize that Christ still has power to bring light to darkened minds, and to cast out the devils which lead to insanity and suicide. When Christ comes into the life he gives peace and calm to the troubled mind, and turns thought away from sin and self to higher things. Shall we not go to those whose minds are upset and bring to them this gospel of sanity? How people need to know that Christ can save their mental life from destruction and ruin! Here is Paul's prescription for a sound mind: "And be not conformed to this world: but be ye transformed by the renewing of your mind, that ye may prove what is that good, and acceptable, and perfect, will of God" (Rom. 12:2).

3. *Salvation Includes the Social Life*

Christ lived as a man among men. He did not withdraw himself from human society, but took a keen interest in the affairs of life. He did not teach us that we are to withdraw ourselves from the world, living apart as hermits, but rather he taught that we are to go out into the world to be its light and its saving salt. To Christ heaven begins here and now. "The kingdom of God," he said, "is within you" (Luke 17: 21). The will of God, he taught us to pray, is to be done on earth as in heaven. The heaven of the hereafter is the completion and the fulfilment of the heaven into which we begin to enter when we become Christians.

Christ's church is a divine-human society which ought to be a sample of heaven on earth. Paul sets up this ideal in Rom. 12: 4-5: "For as we have many members in one body, and all members have not the same office: so we, being many, are one body in Christ, and every one members one of another."

What a different world it would be if this ideal were realized! Every Christian would do the thing he was best fitted for; love would be without deceit; we would abhor that which is evil and cleave to that which is good; we would be kindly affectioned one to another with brotherly love, in honor preferring one another; we would put Christian principles into our everyday living. Let us catch this vision of redeemed people living together, and go out to proclaim with fresh enthusiasm that Christ and Christ only can save our evil social order.

4. *Salvation of the Soul Is All-Inclusive*

Human life is more than the sum total of the physical, mental, and social: it is essentially spiritual. God is Spirit, and when he made us in his image, he made us spiritual beings. By "spirit" or "soul" is meant that eternal part of man which came from God and goes back to God. The soul is the whole personality, which survives bodily death, and which is either forever separated from God because of unforgiven sin or goes to be forever with him because of its redemption through Christ. Christ's supreme concern was for the soul. It is in the saving of the soul that he gives eternal life.

What sort of soul is a saved soul? Paul describes some of its qualities in the remaining verses of the twelfth chapter of Romans. One who is saved is one whom Christ has redeemed from the curse of sin and who is learning from Christ God's way of life. When Christ saves the soul the spirit of the saved man is changed. He learns from his great Master to bless instead of curse his enemies; to be sympathetic and humble; to return good for evil; to be honest in all his dealings; to live at peace with others; to forgive rather than retaliate; to let the Lord have his way in all things. How better could the redeemed spiritual life be summed up than in these final words of Paul's inspired ideal: "Therefore if thine enemy hunger, feed him; if he thirst, give him drink; for in so doing thou shalt heap coals of fire on his head. Be not overcome of evil, but overcome evil with good" (Rom. 12: 20-21).

Thus we see that the salvation of the soul is not something apart from the body, the mind, and the life among men. There is of course no true salvation that is not a salvation of the soul, but in the saving of the soul Christ wants to save all other aspects of the life. When Christ comes into the life and redeems the spirit he becomes the center about which all else revolves. The body becomes the temple of the Holy Spirit, the mind becomes the servant of God, affairs of life become means through which to bring in the heavenly kingdom. The whole of life is thus integrated and harmonized, so that growth in Christlikeness becomes a reality.

What a glorious gospel of salvation this is! What a change would come into the lives of the crippled, the diseased, the mentally disordered, the rebellious and criminal, and the enemies of God, if they only knew and believed this glorious gospel of Christ's salvation for the whole of life!

III. SALVATION FOR TIME AND ETERNITY

In early Christian history there grew up a heathenish practice of putting off baptism until death was near, on the ground that baptism was a washing away of sins, and that it would be wise to wait until there were no more sins to be washed away. Roman Catholics call one of their sacraments "extreme unction," which is administered to the dying in order that soul may be cleansed and better fitted to meet God. A great many people believe that salvation is a sort of insurance policy, the benefits of which cannot be collected until after death.

Everywhere the New Testament emphasizes the truth that the salvation which Christ provides is for the life that *now is*, as well as for the life to come. So through the Gospels you will find Jesus saying again and again, "He that believeth on the Son *hath* everlasting life." The life which Jesus promises is not some faraway, mysterious *future* inheritance, but a *present* possession. Someone has called the Christian life a "present tense salvation." As we seek to bring the life of Christ to the souls of men, let us stress this truth, so needed by and so appealing to the modern mind.

1. *We Are NOW the Children of God*

The apostle John is referred to as "the disciple whom Jesus loved." His was a tender and affectionate nature, and while Jesus no doubt loved all the twelve apostles alike, to John was given a little closer place than to anyone else. We observe this quality of tenderness in John's writings, especially in his epistles.

The Christian community to which John belonged in that first century was a tiny island of the redeemed entirely surrounded by an ocean of heathenism. These Christians were in the world, but they were not of the world. They were linked to each other by strong bonds of common faith and purpose. They had made a great discovery and had entered into a rich experience. John writes to interpret for them the meaning of this new life in Christ.

In the third chapter of his first epistle John reminds these Christians, at this time of discouragement and fierce persecution, of the love of God disclosed in Christ —a love that brings them into the close and loving relationship of children to a Father. Is it any wonder that the unregenerate world should misunderstand and hate them? Such a wicked world knows them not because it knows him not. "Beloved," John affectionately addresses his dear Christian brethren—and us—*"now* are we the sons of God" (1 John 3: 2). That is what it means to be Christians—to enter into a *present* relationship with God as our Father.

2. *We Are NOW Freed from the Curse of Sin*

All sorts of accusations were made against the early Christians. They were compelled to meet secretly to avoid arrest and punishment. These secret meetings gave rise to slander of the vilest character. How could these scandalous false charges best be met? John knew that there was but one way—the Christians must live so completely above reproach that their accusers would be put to shame.

People are not greatly impressed today with claims for Christianity based on magic and mystery. They bluntly ask, "How much better are Christians than those who are not?" By our lives we must prove that Christ frees from the power and the curse of sin, and actually transforms us from the love of self to the love of God and of others. Do not Christians everywhere need to make the witness of pure lives and loving deeds the answer to the world's criticism of Christianity?

3. *We Are NOW to Live the Saved Life*

Someone has suggested that most of us, if we were entirely honest, would pray, "Thy kingdom come . . . but not now!" Do we not all look forward to the time when we are going to live consecrated lives? Have we ever known a lost person who did not expect some time to be saved? Getting us to put off until tomorrow living the Christian life, and waiting for a more convenient season to accept Christ, is the devil's cleverest means of defeating Christ's purposes.

We need to realize that now is the only time that belongs to us. Yesterday is gone and tomorrow has not come. Yesterday was *now* when we had it, and tomorrow will be *now* when it comes. With God all is an eternal *now*. What better time than *today* to put Christ first, and go out to seek to bring someone into his kingdom? What will make some other day a better time to accept Christ than *right now?* We say that "time flies." As a matter of fact it is not time that moves so swiftly on, but life. Time stands still; we move rapidly toward the grave. Before we realize it our lives have sped to their close. Are you forty? Then life is more than half gone! Are you fifty? The sun is beginning to sink rapidly. Are you sixty? Just a few more years left!

Oh, how we ought to make these last years count! John, who wrote this wonderful chapter we are studying, is said to have lived to be a hundred years old. Right up to the end he witnessed for Christ. Tradition has it that when he was too feeble to walk he would be brought on a couch to where the persecuted Christians were meeting, and spreading out his hands in blessing would say, "Little children, love one another!" Are we so living *now* that old age will find us sweet and happy and useful?

4. *Eternity Is NOW in Our Hearts*

What is the final and sufficient evidence of eternity in the heart? Just two simple things, John tells us: First, that we believe on the name of God's Son, Jesus Christ; and, second, that we love one another. This sums up the Christian life in two short sentences. This is the "new commandment" revealed in Christ which fulfils and replaces all the others. Out of this great twofold spiritual law all other commandments grow. "And he that keepeth his commandments dwelleth in him, and he in him. And hereby we know that he abideth in us, by the Spirit which he hath given us" (1 John 3:24).

IV. SALVATION FOR ALL MEN EVERYWHERE

1. *The Shadow That Falls Across the World*

Across the world, nineteen centuries ago, a dark and terrible shadow had fallen. The religion of the Jews had apparently failed. God had covenanted with Abraham to make of him a great nation, to bless him, and to make his name great. In him, the divine promise ran, all families of the earth should be blessed. The centuries had come and gone, and the Israel of God had been scattered. The Promised Land had been spoiled, and had come under the cruel dominion of tyrannical Rome. Fierce dictators ruled the earth, war brought its blight and ruin, and the multitudes were hungry, poverty-stricken and depressed. It looked as if the darkness of night was settling over mankind.

In this century two global wars have shaken the world. The questions are asked, Has Christianity failed? Must we give up hope of the coming of God's kingdom? Is the vision of a redeemed humanity, in which there shall be brotherhood and peace, an empty dream which will never come true? While billions are being poured into war debts, other billions are being spent in rehabilitation of ruined cities and villages. In China our Christian churches, schools, and hospitals were ruthlessly destroyed. The job of rebuilding may take many years, but it is going forward with all speed. Almost as terrible as warfare with instruments of destruction is the economic and political warfare in which we are still engaged. At such a time does not the message of the angelic chorus, "Glory to God in the highest, and on earth peace, good will toward men" sung at the birth of Christ need to be proclaimed as never before? Peace will not finally come until "the earth shall be full of the knowledge of the Lord, as the waters cover the sea" (Isa. 11: 9). Can we not with confidence believe that God is steadfastly working his purpose out for the salvation of this lost world in which we live?

2. *The Promise of a Glorious Dawn*

Do you not like to watch the sun come up? Perhaps you have waited through a weary night of suffering for the day to dawn. How blessed it is to realize with what absolute certainty we can count on the night giving way to day! Zacharias, in his prophecy concerning the Holy Child soon to be born, compared his coming to the sunrise. His birth, Zacharias declared, would be in order "to give knowledge of salvation unto his people by the remission of their sins," and this mighty truth would dawn upon the world as when the sun rises, through the tender mercy of our God; whereby "the dayspring from on high hath visited us." (See Luke 1:77-78.)

Since Christ came the world has never been, and can never be, in such spiritual darkness as it was before his birth. The Sun of Righteousness has risen and this Sun will never set. But there are deep caverns into which the light of this Sun has not penetrated; and there are dark clouds which sometimes shut off the full light of this Sun from men. It is our business who have the light to take it into these dark places, and to dispel the clouds which sometimes dim its brightness. What we must never forget is that there is light enough for all, but that we must bring those who are in darkness unto the light.

3. *Light for All Who Sit in Darkness*

Why was Jesus born? Zacharias gives the answer: "To give light to them that sit in darkness and in the shadow of death, to guide our feet into the way of peace" (Luke 1: 79). A house may be on a sunny hill, but those within may sit in darkness because the windows are all closed and the shades tightly drawn. We are not the Light, as John declared that he was not the Light; but we have seen the Light, and we are bidden to go to all men everywhere and tell them of the Light. We are to bring them the good news that Christ is the "true Light, which lighteth every man that cometh into the world." It is our mission to persuade those who sit in darkness to throw open the windows, and to open wide the doors, and let the Light of Life shine in. Darkness means death, for nothing can live without light. Jesus said, "I am the light of the world," and without him the souls of men everywhere must die.

What would Christ do for us today? It is he and he alone who can "guide our feet into the way of peace." How can that peace be found? Not through temples or sacrifices, or creeds or rituals; not through armies and navies, nor through peace treaties and world courts. There is but one pathway to peace, for the individual and for the nations, and that is through him who is "the way, the truth, and the life."

QUESTIONS FOR REVIEW AND CLASS DISCUSSION

1. Do you believe that there could come a worldwide revival in our generation that would bring multitudes of every nation into the kingdom of God? What hinders it? What would make it possible?

2. Are there any "hopeless cases"—sinners so degraded or hardened that Christ could not save them? Give an instance of Christ's power to save the worst of men.

3. If you were to pick out one thing above another, what would you say is the chief reason why men and women reject Christ today? What surrender must the sinner make before Christ will receive him?

4. What is included when it is said that salvation is for the whole of life? How does being a Christian aid in maintaining physical health?

5. What are some chief causes of mental breakdown today? How does living the Christian life help to preserve a sound mind?

6. When does heaven begin for the Christian? How does Christianity propose to make earth like unto heaven?

7. What is the best proof to an unbelieving world that we are *now* the children of God? What manner of life should be ours if we are saved both for time and eternity?

8. Why do we put off to some future time living consecrated lives and going forth to win others? How many years do you think you have left? What do you expect to do for Christ during these remaining years?

9. Upon what does your hope rest that Christ will prevail and there will at last be peace on earth, good will among men?

10. What is God's purpose in Christ for our world? What is the place of Christian missions in God's redemptive plan? How are you proving your loyalty to Christ through devotion to the missionary enterprise?

QUESTIONS FOR REVIEW AND EXAMINATION

For instructions concerning the examination and the requesting of awards, see Directions for the Teaching and the Study of This Book for Credit, page 7.

CHAPTER I

1. In its broadest sense, what is *evangelism?* What are some inadequate forms of evangelism? What kind of evangelism do we most need today?
2. What temptations especially beset us today? What is our hope of overcoming these temptations?
3. What are the terrible consequences of sin? What certain punishment does sin bring?
4. When one becomes a Christian, does he instantly attain to perfection of character? How is Christian character achieved?
5. Why is sound Christian character of utmost importance in soul-winning? What is the source of our power and influence in winning others to Christ?

CHAPTER II

6. What three main lessons concerning evangelism do we learn from a study of Pentecost?
7. In Christ's plan, who are to do the witnessing? How account for the fact that so few members of a typical Baptist church are soul-winners?
8. What are the three main ways in which a church can best fulfil its commission to witness? In what ways do you feel that you can best do your part?
9. Give several ways by which a church can attract the unsaved to its preaching and teaching services.
10. Which is more important in successful evangelism, preaching or personal work? Why should they always go together?

CHAPTER III

11. Suppose someone should ask, "Just what do you mean by 'salvation'?" Give your answer in a few words.

12. What is "grace"? Why is it impossible for anyone to deserve salvation or to be saved because of good works and character?

13. Why is faith necessary to salvation? Are we saved by something we believe or by Christ in whom we believe?

14. What is repentance? What are the evidences of true repentance? Why is repentance necessary to salvation?

15. What is Christian obedience? Give a half-dozen ways in which the Christian should obey Christ. What are the rewards of obedience?

CHAPTER IV

16. What are some of the dangers that threaten home life today? What are some of the consequences when the home fails?

17. Why should Christians take an active part in politics? State a half-dozen obligations of the Christian citizen.

18. How would you state the doctrine of stewardship? Why should a person have the duty of giving made plain while he is being won to Christ?

19. To what does "stewardship" refer besides money? How are we to discharge our stewardship of faithful testimony?

20. What is our guilt if souls whom we should have brought to Christ perish? How does the Holy Spirit help us to be good witnesses?

CHAPTER V

21. Give what you consider a half-dozen most necessary qualifications for becoming a skilful soul-winner.

22. What are some of the mistakes to be avoided in approaching an individual about becoming a Christian? Give briefly an example of how you would undertake to make the approach.

23. How would you go about finding what is the real barrier between the soul and the Saviour? Who should do most of the talking? What is the danger of argument?

24. What shall you do when the individual agrees with you, but wants to delay decision? Why is it not wise to overpersuade?

25. Should the person with whom you are dealing accept Christ as Saviour, but object to public confession and joining the church, what would you say?

CHAPTER VI

26. Is the Christian religion, on the whole, winning or losing in our day? Give two reasons for encouragement and two reasons for discouragement.

27. Where do the worldly crowds flock? What attitude shall we take toward those who heedlessly refuse to give any attention to God's day, God's house, God's love, Christ's message?

28. Suppose one with whom you are dealing should express doubt of God's existence. How would you undertake to prove that there is a God? What sort of God would you show him to be?

29. List three or four practical difficulties that come between men and Christ. State in a few words how these difficulties are to be overcome.

30. How may the Christian worker best prepare himself to deal with the many forms of doubt and difficulty that keep people from Christ today?

CHAPTER VII

31. In answer to the question, What kind of revival do we need? List five marks of the sort of revival you would like to see come to your church.

32. What are the advantages of the Sunday school which make it the most efficient soul-winning agency of the church?

33. What twofold part should the Baptist Training Union play in the church's evangelistic program? How can your training Union be made more fruitful for evangelism?

34. Why is it supremely important to win Intermediates and young people? What is the danger if they pass into adulthood unsaved? Tell how you would go about the winning of an unsaved young person.

35. Why is it so difficult to win adults to Christ? Give five of the most valuable suggestions as to how to present Christ to adults.

Chapter VIII

36. If you were to pick out one thing above another, what would you say is the chief reason why men and women reject Christ today? What surrender must the sinner make before Christ will receive him?

37. What is included when it is said that salvation is for the whole of life? How does being a Christian aid in maintaining physical health?

38. What is the best proof to an unbelieving world that we are *now* the children of God? What manner of life should be ours if we are saved both for time and eternity?

39. Upon what does your hope rest that Christ will prevail and there will at last be peace on earth, good will among men?

40. What is God's purpose in Christ for our world? What is the place of Christian missions in God's redemptive plan? How are you proving your loyalty to Christ through devotion to the missionary enterprise?

Date Due

Code 436-279, CLS-4, Broadman Supplies, Nashville, Tenn., Printed in U.S.A.